L.E.A.P.
27

L.E.A.P. 27

IMMANUEL

TATE PUBLISHING
AND ENTERPRISES, LLC

L.E.A.P. 27
Copyright © 2015 by IMMANUEL. All rights reserved.

No part of this publication may be reproduced, stored in a retrieval system or transmitted in any way by any means, electronic, mechanical, photocopy, recording or otherwise without the prior permission of the author except as provided by USA copyright law.

Scripture quotations marked (AMP) are taken from the *Amplified Bible*, Copyright © 1954, 1958, 1962, 1964, 1965, 1987 by The Lockman Foundation. Used by permission.

Scripture quotations marked (ESV) are from *The Holy Bible, English Standard Version®*, copyright © 2001 by Crossway Bibles, a publishing ministry of Good News Publishers. Used by permission. All rights reserved.

Scripture quotations marked (KJV) are taken from the *Holy Bible, King James Version*, Cambridge, 1769. Used by permission. All rights reserved.

Scripture quotations marked (NIV) are taken from the *Holy Bible, New International Version®*, NIV®. Copyright © 1973, 1978, 1984 by Biblica, Inc.™ Used by permission of Zondervan. All rights reserved worldwide. www.zondervan.com

Scripture quotations marked (NKJV) are taken from the *New King James Version*. Copyright © 1982 by Thomas Nelson, Inc. Used by permission. All rights reserved.

Scripture quotations marked (NLT) are taken from the *Holy Bible, New Living Translation*, copyright © 1996. Used by permission of Tyndale House Publishers, Inc., Wheaton, Illinois 60189. All rights reserved.

This book is designed to provide accurate and authoritative information with regard to the subject matter covered. This information is given with the understanding that neither the author nor Tate Publishing, LLC is engaged in rendering legal, professional advice. Since the details of your situation are fact dependent, you should additionally seek the services of a competent professional.

The opinions expressed by the author are not necessarily those of Tate Publishing, LLC.

Published by Tate Publishing & Enterprises, LLC
127 E. Trade Center Terrace | Mustang, Oklahoma 73064 USA
1.888.361.9473 | www.tatepublishing.com

Tate Publishing is committed to excellence in the publishing industry. The company reflects the philosophy established by the founders, based on Psalm 68:11,

"The Lord gave the word and great was the company of those who published it."

Book design copyright © 2015 by Tate Publishing, LLC. All rights reserved.
Cover design by Joseph Emnace
Interior design by Manolito Bastasa

Published in the United States of America

ISBN: 978-1-68028-313-6
1. Religion / Christian Life / Love & Marriage
2. Religion / Biblical Meditations / General
15.05.11

To my son Brendan, wife, kids, and grandfather

Acknowledgments

To my son Brendan Isaiah, whom I will always hold close to my heart no matter what, you have endured a lot of hardships from me, my son. I told you Daddy would conquer this evil, and in Jesus's mighty name, I did. I love you so dearly, and it is truly because of your hope in me that this book is made possible. Jesus truly heard your prayers.

To my wife, if it wasn't for you true strength in life, I would have fallen to the overbearing fear of not being able to conquer my fears. It was your prayers, support, love, compassion, determination, and, most importantly, your trust in God that he could and would change this man for the better. How do I begin to tell you how lucky I am to have you in my life? I'll start by saying what a gift you gave me the day you became my wife. I love you with all my heart and soul. I thought that you should know but from time to time you don't think I mean it... how this can be ever so. You mean the world to me and you constantly light up my day. You touch my heart deep inside in an everlasting and unimaginable way. I thought that my life was over before you unlocked my heart. But when I thought it was the end you showed me where I could begin to start. You're my best friend in the good times and my rock in times of sorrow. You're the reason for sweet yesterdays and my promise for tomorrow. It makes me feel comfort when you are with me and always by my side. My love that I have for you is obvious and something I cannot hide. The love that I have for you is undoubtedly pure and the absolute truth. Time will age me inevitably, but you in this life are and will always be my fountain of youth. Since I have been with you… my view on life is clear, God gave me you for all my trials to come so I can persevere. I am willing to give my life for you, yes my one and only life, a sacrifice worth giving up to my one and only wife.

To the family who never could understand what it took for this man to become this better man. I love you so dearly in which you stood boldly beside me even in my darkest hour.

To the friends in my life whom I will always love the most, it was because of you that kept me going. You had a choice to abandon me when times were tough, but you always seemed to stand by me no matter the outcome.

To the alcohol that tried to bind to my soul and to the drugs that tried to cloud my mind and control my personal well-being, if it weren't for your true deception, I would have never found my one true calling. I will tell you this: this world can tell me who I was supposed to be, but my Savior, Jesus Christ, told me that I was never meant to be. We all need to stop taking detours in our lives and find the true direction through Christ.

So in closing, it will not be until my death, which is predestined to come my way, will I ever stop proclaiming the name of the Lord. I will always choose to walk with God in this life; that's my choice and what I will choose today and forevermore.

Contents

Foreword... 11

Introduction.. 17

Where Is God? 41

A Letter from Deceit.. 43

LEAP 27 Contract 45

PART I

SEVEN DAYS OF BUILDING YOUR FOUNDATION AND BLUEPRINT

1 Fasting/Old You—Destroy Your Temple 47

2 Building the New You 61

3 Love Everyone... 73

4 Enjoy Every Moment 83

5 Accept Any Situation 93

6 Praise God and Give Peace.. 103

7 Faith with Good Deeds 111

PART II

SEVEN DAYS OF BUILDING YOUR STRUCTURE

1 Armor of God 121

2 Holy Spirit 133

3 Living by the Spirit's Power.. 143

4	Spiritual Gifts	151
5	Teaching How to Pray	161
6	Words of Authority	173
7	Good Samaritan	183

PART III

Seven Days of Recognizing the Stumbling Block

1	The Birth and Recognition of Sin	191
2	Conflict Within Us	203
3	Knowing Your Enemy	211
4	Trials and Tribulations	221
5	Satan's Fall	229
6	World Views	237
7	God Gives	245
8	God's Plan	251

PART IV

Five Days of Getting Ready to Show Your New Structure

1	God's Promise	257
2	Follow by Example	267
3	Peter and You	275
4	Time for Everything	283

PART V

Grand Opening

| 1 | Watchmen (Testify, It's Your Turn Now) | 291 |

| About the Author | 299 |

Foreword

February 17, 2012, is a date I can never forget. That was the date my grandfather passed away, early that the morning. That same day was the day that my life would change forever. That was the day that I drank my life to oblivion and was arrested for DUI. I was never able to get out of jail to attend my grandfather's funeral. He was the man who was a true leader in my life. He tried so hard to raise me the best way that he could. It's painful to my soul how a man who made a substantial impact in my heart had to die in order for me to be reborn into the person I am today. While he was alive, he tried very hard to change the lifestyle that I was living, but it never sunk in. On that dreadful day, I learned a very important lesson, a lesson that even in death my grandfather could never stop teaching me. Sometimes it takes a tragedy in one's life in order to have victory to others. He has been teaching me this lesson all my life through the teaching and life of Jesus Christ, but it never stuck to my soul until I witnessed it in his death.

It was in jail where I found my only one true Savior, Jesus Christ. Was this the man, the Savior that my grandfather was speaking of all these years? I remember on March 9, 2012, I had one of the strangest dreams that would transform my life, my soul, and fill my spirit forever. It was in that dream that I realized it was more than just a dream; it was a revelation to my new well-being. This was to be a vision given to me from God, but I never knew what he was telling me until this book. I would like to share that dream, that vision, with you verbatim with what I wrote the next morning on paper. I did not change the words to the paper at all. As a matter of fact, it is exact, even if the words are misspelled. I did not alter this part of the book for God's true message to be revealed:

DREAM MARCH 9, 2012

I was in a shcool setting. I was still conscious of being in jail though. I made a phone call to my mother. I was disappointed because no one has come to visit me. I remember not being able to talk on the phone because it was a collect call, but I could hear her voice. She told me that to be patient and I get out on Sunday or a couple of days later. Then I exited the phone boothe and chased after a bus. Not sure why though. I think I was traveling somewhere. The bus was driving off so I chased it and finally made it inside. I asked the driver to turn back around because I was getting out. He turned back around, then dropped me off at the school. For some reason there was people dieing at this school and I realized a connection. They all died at the same exact time. 2:00 am in the morning. Then I tried to find the killer and took a piece of paper or cloth, not really sure and waited for 2:00 am. Finally it came and I saw a portal open before my eyes. I ran to the portal and shoved the paper into it. The paper engulfed the being that was coming through the portal trapping it. I then folded the paper to keep it sealed inside. I squeezed my right hand tightly because the spirit was trying to escape. My right hand was as bright as a light. All I could think about was help. So I ran inside and saw a preacher. I ran up to him asking him for his help. Pleading with him because I didn't know what to do. The preacher was with some people and he got scared and told me to leave there was nothing he could do for me. Then he ran. I was alone and helpless. I ran outside and looked up at the sky. I saw a fish shape pattern in the sky. Kind of looked like this (had a fish drawing on the original document). Then that opened my eyes. As the spirit started to flow down my arm I fell to my knees and screamed out My Lord Jesus' name. Then I saw a light in front of me. It was a man, (The Son of God), my savior Jesus Christ holding his arms open. I knew what he wanted. I ran as fast as I could and I ran into his arms. He grasped me firmly and I finally felt peace and was safe. Then the bright light covered my eyes. Then I awoke with a woman holding me, not sure who she was and my son holding me. Then I awoke…I felt a wonderful love of Christ inside of me. The love, compassion, peace, joy, and happiness. I prayed and continued my day.

MEANING

When God revealed the true meaning of this dream it wasn't until two years later, but was a remarkable revelation. There were children dying in my dream and I compared it to the children dying right now as we speak. In this world there are too many kids having kids, kids raising kids, and finally kids killing kids and that is plainly unacceptable. Jesus wanted us to raise and protect our children and he is very disappointed in our actions. The world has given this generation a name. *GENERATION X,* a generation of rejects and failures is what we are being told. Jesus said in Luke 23:34 "Father, forgive them for they do not know what they are doing." Do we truly understand this statement? Do we truly love Gods children? Or do we naturally rebuke the children of this world for their incompetence on life just as Jesus disciples did?

And they brought unto him also infants, that he would touch them: but when his disciples saw it, they rebuked

IMMANUEL

them. But Jesus called them unto him, and said, suffer little children to come unto me, and forbid them not: for of such is the kingdom of God. Verily I say unto you, Whosoever shall not receive the kingdom of God as a little child shall in no wise enter therein. (Luke 18:15–17, KJV)

I truly believe by the end of this book we will start an uprising in order to change our generation of rejects to a generation of righteousness for humanity who will become servants of Jesus Christ. They will be as strong as fiery lights, and their mouths shall be full of blessings. It will be at the end of this book that the righteousness will flow before every person as water and will not withhold the wisdom given by the Lord. This will be received according to the trials and tribulations in our life. It is through these countless experiences that God will strengthen his Holy Spirit that dwells in those who call upon it. It will make known the darkness of sinners and bring them to light of righteousness. This will be truly a new generation to come.

As for the paper in the dream, God spoke to me about that paper that was stuck in the portal and trapped was the book *LEAP 27*. This book is crawling with the Holy Spirit and is waiting to be released inside you. As the Spirit rose all throughout my body, no one understood what was going on, so they rejected me. This is truly what is happening today. When you complete this book, it will also happen to you. This book is an ultimate transformation in a way that God meant for it to be. Don't be afraid of the light as it creeps deep inside of you. At the end of this book, I promise you will have a sense of wonder you have never experienced before in your life. Don't let your pride or your wisdom keep you from what God truly wants you to know. You will come to a spiritual conclusion at the end of this book that will make you appreciate an indefinite moral modification your soul has been yearning for. You will begin to understand that your body will surely die, your spirit will surely rise, but the message of God revealed through this book and in you will always be ALIVE.

May the God of Abraham and Moses be with you on your journey. May his Son given to you by his grace, Jesus Christ, who died for your sins be by your side in love. May Christ send you the Holy Spirit, who will lead you through all your trials as you read this book. I pray all of this in Jesus Christ's mighty name. Amen.

Introduction

What is LEAP 27?

*L*ove everybody.
*E*njoy every moment in life.
*A*ccept any situation.
*P*raise God, and peace to everyone.

This is the most resilient mantra that you will live by for the next twenty-seven days. It is important to memorize it and keep it close to your heart. You will have to tell yourself these four simple sayings every day from the moment you awake till the moment you lie down to rest. Your way of thinking has to be challenged every moment in order to turn your life around. Later in the book, you will learn and understand the in-depth meaning of each section of LEAP. For right now, it is important to memorize it and recite it to yourself over and over. When you confess it out loud, you plant the seed in your heart. Once that seed is planted, your own confession every day will nourish your mantra, and you will start turning your words into actions. Here you will learn to control your own individual emotions rather than letting your emotions control the individual. "Intellect makes the best decisions in life, while our emotions make the worst ones" (author unknown).

When you make your everyday decisions based on emotions, sometimes the outcome of that situation could be severe, or even fatal. When this happens, you tend to think of the five most important questions that only you can answer:

1. Who did this?
2. What was I thinking?
3. When did this happen?
4. Where was my mind?
5. Why did I lose control?

After that last question is when you realize it is too late. The action has already substantially taken place, and now it is time to face the reaction of the consequences. But there is and has always been another way!

Love Everybody

Why should I love everyone?

You cannot control every person you come in contact with or the way they think. All you can control is your own decisions and actions. You don't have to like what they do, but by God's true standard you need to learn to just love them instead. This book will demonstrate a huge display of abundant love coming from you to give to others through your own activities for others.

> By this we know love, because He laid down His life for us. And we also ought to lay down our lives for the brethren. But whoever has this world's goods, and sees his brother in need, and shuts up his heart from him, how does the love of God abide in him? My little children, let us not love in word or in tongue, but in deed and in truth. (1 John 3:16–18, NKJV)

Do I truly love God, or does God truly love me? This question is a very hard question to answer. You may think it is by your decision that God should show you mercy and love, but in reality, it is by God's own mercy and grace toward His creation that is the reason He loves us.

> And God said, Let us make man in our image, after our likeness: and let them have dominion over the fish of the sea, and over the fowl of the air, and over the cattle, and over all the earth, and over every creeping thing that creepeth upon the earth. So God created man in his own image, in the image of God created he him; male and female created he them. (Genesis 1:26–27, KJV)

> Beloved, if God so loved us, we ought also to love one another. No man hath seen God at any time. If we love one another, God dwelleth in us, and his love is perfected in us. (1 John 4:11–12, KJV)

> A new commandment I give unto you, That ye love one another; as I have loved you, that ye also love one another. By this shall all men know that ye are my disciples, if ye have love one to another. (John 13:34–35, KJV)

You need to stop treating love as an emotion or even worse, just a word, and turn it into an action. It is in that action that you will learn that like is the emotion and you don't have to like what people do, but you must love them because we are all God's children created in his own image.

Enjoy Every Moment in Life

Is it truly possible to enjoy a life in Christ?

You cannot control every single moment in life, so just enjoy the moment for what it is, swift and in an instant and that no matter what happens, good or bad, the time will surely pass. Unless you can control time, slow down time when the good comes and speed up time when the bad comes, in which you can't this book will show what an actual enjoyment of each moment is in life.

> That you may fear the Lord your God, to keep all His statutes and His commandments which I command you, you and your son and your grandson, all the days of your life, and that your days may be prolonged. (Deuteronomy 6:2, NKJV)

> God has delivered me from going down to the pit, and I shall live to enjoy the light of life.' God does all these things to a person—twice, even three times—to turn them back from the pit, that the light of life may shine on them. (Job 33:28–30, NIV)

> There is nothing better for a man, than that he should eat and drink, and that he should make his soul enjoy good in his labour. This also I saw, that it was from the hand of God. For who can eat, or who else can hasten hereunto, more than I? (Ecclesiastes 2:24–25, KJV)

> A man to whom God has given riches, possessions, and honor, so that he lacks nothing for his soul of all that he might desire, yet God does not give him the power or capacity to enjoy them [things which are gifts from God], but a stranger [in whom he has no interest succeeds him and] consumes and enjoys them. This is vanity (emptiness, falsity, and futility); it is a sore affliction! (Ecclesiastes 6:2, AMP)

Accept Any Situation

Why should I accept any situation?

You cannot control every situation that comes your way, so you just need learn to accept them wholeheartedly. You have been taught that there is always an easy way out of any situation, but in this book it will respectably show you how to just accept uncontrollable situations in your heart and embrace it, not run from it.

> But he said unto her, Thou speakest as one of the foolish women speaketh. What? shall we receive good at the hand of God, and shall we not receive evil? In all this did not Job sin with his lips. (Job 2:10, KJV)

> My son, if you receive my words, And treasure my commands within you, So that you incline your ear to wisdom, And apply your heart to understanding; Yes, if you cry out for discernment,
> And lift up your voice for understanding, If you seek her as silver, And search for her as for hidden treasures; Then you will understand the fear of the Lord,
> And find the knowledge of God. For the Lord gives wisdom; From His mouth come knowledge and understanding; He stores up sound wisdom for the upright; He is a shield to those who walk uprightly; He guards the paths of justice, And preserves the way of His saints. Then you will understand righteousness and justice, Equity and every good path. (Proverbs 2:1–9, NKJV)

> And it is a good thing to receive wealth from God and the good health to enjoy it. To enjoy your work and accept your lot in life—this is indeed a gift from God. God keeps such people so busy enjoying life that they take no time to brood over the past. (Ecclesiastes 5:19–20, NLT)

Praise God and Give Peace to Everyone

And the final and most significant piece of the mantra: praise God and give peace to everyone. In this book you will learn that

IMMANUEL

by loving others unconditionally, enjoying the moments in life completely, and accepting all and every situation unquestionably, you are giving praise to God in the highest form possible.

> I create the fruit of the lips; Peace, peace to him that is far off, and to him that is near, saith the Lord; and I will heal him. (Isaiah 57:19, KJV)

> And [Jerusalem] shall be to Me a name of joy, a praise and a glory before all the nations of the earth that hear of all the good I do for it, and they shall fear and tremble because of all the good and all the peace, prosperity, security, and stability I provide for it. (Jeremiah 33:9, AMP)

Do you see how very plain and simple it is? In just these four sayings, you are going to test your personality as well as make the modifications you need by looking at your existence from a whole new perspective.

With these four God-based thoughts are planted in your heart and are constantly being nourished, your personal stress level in life will decrease abundantly as for the happiness in life will increase significantly in Jesus Christ's mighty name. Don't take our word for it. Why don't you take a look at what the Word of God shows you about this subject?

> And he answering said, Thou shalt love the Lord thy God with all thy heart, and with all thy soul, and with all thy strength, and with all thy mind; and thy neighbour as thyself. (Luke 10:27, KJV)

> Jesus said unto him, Thou shalt love the Lord thy God with all thy heart, and with all thy soul, and with all thy mind. This is the first and great commandment. (Matthew 22:37–38, KJV)

And thou shalt love the Lord thy God with all thy heart, and with all thy soul, and with all thy mind, and with all thy strength: this is the first commandment. (Mark 12:30, KJV)

And thou shalt love the Lord thy God with all thine heart, and with all thy soul, and with all thy might. (Deuteronomy 6:5, KJV)

Is it starting to become obvious on why you are not receiving the full blessings of God that is meant for you? In this trifecta God-based program, you will learn to overcome the complexities of this world and grasp the simplicities of your life the way God intended for it to be. It all starts with sustaining your soul, then feeding your mind, and, finally, nourishing your body. God is ready to complete you, but are you ready to make the change?

Do not love the world or the things in the world. If anyone loves the world, the love of the Father is not in him. For all that is in the world—*the lust of the flesh, the lust of the eyes, and the pride of life*—is not of the Father but is of the world. And the world is passing away, and the lust of it; but he who does the will of God abides forever. (1 John 2:15–17, NKJV; emphasis mine)

In the above passage, notice the italicized area: "The lust of the flesh, the lust of the eyes, and the pride of life."

When you lust of the flesh, this could refer to the following:

- Drugs or alcohol
- Money
- People
- Materials or objects

Your only outcome will be to lose control of your body.

IMMANUEL

When you lust of the eyes, this could refer to the following:

- Television
- Magazines
- Video games
- People

Your only outcome will be to lose control of your mind.

When you take pride of your life, this could refer to the following:

- One's own dignity
- One's own importance
- One's own value
- One's own morals

Your only outcome will be to lose control of your soul.

Do you notice the order on how you lose control of the battle within? It starts with your body, works toward your mind, and finally, you will lose your soul. In this way, it is truly inevitable not to lose total control of who you are. These are the reasons behind the way you feel at life without a purpose. Your existence without a purpose is the same as having a purpose without actually existing. Your happiness cannot ever exist unless you discover what you were created to do by God. In this program, you will learn to reverse the sequence so you can take back your sanity and regain what is rightfully yours. That is your life in Jesus Christ. This will be the foundation of your well-being. Here, you will sit back and let God take control of your life and do what He has planned to do since you were born.

> You watched me as I was being formed in utter seclusion,
> as I was woven together in the dark of the womb. You saw
> me before I was born. Every day of my life was recorded in

your book. Every moment was laid out before a single day had passed. (Psalms 139:15–16, NLT)

God is the architect of your design of life, Jesus Christ is the blueprint to your soul, your body is the foundation, and your mind is the completed structure that is being built. You cannot lack any of these special qualities, or the structure will not be sturdy, with the devastating truth that in the end your foundation will eventually come collapsing down.

What is the purpose of this book?

> To know wisdom and instruction; to perceive the words of understanding; To receive the instruction of wisdom, justice, and judgment, and equity; To give subtilty to the simple, to the young man knowledge and discretion. A wise man will hear, and will increase learning; and a man of understanding shall attain unto wise counsels: To understand a proverb, and the interpretation; the words of the wise, and their dark sayings. The fear of the Lord is the beginning of knowledge: but fools despise wisdom and instruction. (Proverbs 1:2–7, KJV)

Not everyone will be able to do what this program has to offer. How can you know if you can do this program? You must ask yourself can I be of honesty, not with another but with myself before God. You must break away all that you were taught in trying to find comfort in illusionary honesty with another person and first find transparent honesty with God, who sees all you do. Now I do promise you the one great thing about this book, and it is our guarantee to you: "If you are not completely satisfied with the results after the 27 days of this dynamic program, we guarantee your misery back."

Enough said; now you have nothing to lose and everything to gain. It is time for you to take everything this book has to offer

| 25 |

you and give back all of the wisdom you learn to others. Now ask yourself these two important questions: "How long have I been miserable in my life?" and "Can I truly be happy after reading this book?" Take a look at the answer that lies within this book and what you will be doing for the next 27 vigorous days. This can and will lead you toward your one true glory and happiness in life.

Soul

> I say then: Walk in the Spirit, and you shall not fulfill the lust of the flesh. For the flesh lusts against the Spirit, and the Spirit against the flesh; and these are contrary to one another, so that you do not do the things that you wish. But if you are led by the Spirit, you are not under the law. Now the works of the flesh are evident, which are: adultery, fornication, uncleanness, lewdness, idolatry, sorcery, hatred, contentions, jealousies, outbursts of wrath, selfish ambitions, dissensions, heresies, envy, murders, drunkenness, revelries, and the like; of which I tell you beforehand, just as I also told you in time past, that those who practice such things will not inherit the kingdom of God. But the fruit of the Spirit is love, joy, peace, longsuffering, kindness, goodness, faithfulness, gentleness, self–control. Against such there is no law. And those who are Christ's have crucified the flesh with its passions and desires. If we live in the Spirit, let us also walk in the Spirit. Let us not become conceited, provoking one another, envying one another. (Galatians 5:16–26, NKJV)

Your soul is the blueprint of life. Without a design of what you are going to build, how can you know what is being created and why? Here you will learn how to align your soul with Jesus Christ by reading, studying, and meditating on the Word of God. It is important that you spend time reading the Bible so you can complete each detailed design in your blueprint, then study what you just read, and finally meditate on Gods word which is given to you by the architect (God). In each day of this program, you will discover a new portion of your life that lies dormant inside you and is just waiting to be found. It is like a treasure hunt for your soul. Out of all the three sections in your design—your mind, body, and soul—it is your soul that is the most difficult to maintain in order to fulfill a healthy lifestyle. Living a life through Jesus Christ is not easy. As a matter of fact, this is a road that is hard and rough that you have to train for but has a gift that will last an eternity.

> Enter by the narrow gate; for wide is the gate and broad is the way that leads to destruction, and there are many who go in by it. Because narrow is the gate and difficult is the way which leads to life, and there are few who find it. (Matthew 7:13–14, NKJV)

Would you just throw on some football pads and a Dallas Cowboys jersey and expect to play in the NFL? Or better yet, would you just throw on some running shoes and go run a 25-mile marathon without any kind of training and expect to win? Of course you wouldn't, and in this same sense, you can't have a perfect walk with Christ without suffering blood, sweat, and tears. You truly have to train your soul so when the time comes, you will be skilled and prepared for what the devil will hurl at you.

> Beloved, do not be amazed and bewildered at the fiery ordeal which is taking place to test your quality, as though something strange (unusual and alien to you and your position) were befalling you. But insofar as you are sharing Christ's sufferings, rejoice, so that when His glory [full of radiance and splendor] is revealed, you may also rejoice with triumph [exultantly]. If you are censured and suffer abuse [because you bear] the name of Christ, blessed [are you—happy, fortunate, to be envied, with life–joy, and sat-

isfaction in God's favor and salvation, regardless of your outward condition], because the Spirit of glory, the Spirit of God, is resting upon you. On their part He is blasphemed, but on your part He is glorified. But let none of you suffer as a murderer or a thief or any sort of criminal, or as a mischief–maker (a meddler) in the affairs of others [infringing on their rights]. But if [one is ill-treated and suffers] as a Christian [which he is contemptuously called], let him not be ashamed, but give glory to God that he is [deemed worthy to suffer] in this name. For the time [has arrived] for judgment to begin with the household of God; and if it begins with us, what will [be] the end of those who do not respect or believe or obey the good news (the Gospel) of God? And if the righteous are barely saved, what will become of the godless and wicked? Therefore, those who are ill–treated and suffer in accordance with God's will must do right and commit their souls [in charge as a deposit] to the One Who created [them] and will never fail [them]. (1 Peter 4:12–19, AMP)

This is the part of the transformation that a lot of people are afraid of and rightfully so. The soul is the most sought after peace of the human anatomy by many scholars and yet cannot seem to find. The reality of it is this, you will always hide behind a mask of lies, but your one true soul lies with-in the sparks of every decision you make on a daily basis. The trials and tribulations are just a part of growth in Jesus Christ. Here are a couple of questions that will be answered by God's Word.

What if I fail Christ?

And if anyone hears My words and does not believe, I do not judge him; for I did not come to judge the world but to save the world. (John 12:47, NKJV)

Jesus Christ didn't come here to condemn you for your failures but to save you. As a matter of fact it will take all your failures in life to create 100% faith in God. Only when you fail 100% and lose all faith in yourself, can you put all of your faith in Jesus. Jesus can do anything for you if you will have 100% faith in Him. Your failures do not determine the ending, just the beginning of our true success in Jesus. That is an important factor you must remember when you are being faced with any problems of the world. Jesus is here to conquer your problems with you and not scorn you for failing.

What if I am not ready?

> Dear brothers and sisters, when I was with you I couldn't talk to you as I would to spiritual people. I had to talk as though you belonged to this world or as though you were infants in the Christian life. I had to feed you with milk, not with solid food, because you weren't ready for anything stronger. And you still aren't ready, for you are still controlled by your sinful nature. You are jealous of one another and quarrel with each other. Doesn't that prove you are controlled by your sinful nature? Aren't you living like people of the world? (1 Corinthians 3:1–3, NLT)

Are you poor in spirit? Are you the one who mourns? Are you humble and gentle? Are you one who has hunger and thirst for righteousness? Are you merciful? Are you pure in heart? Are you peacemakers? Are you persecuted because of righteousness? Are you insulted, persecuted, and hearing false things said of you? Then you will definitely be ready when the time comes. You have to take the baby steps that are necessary in order to walk. Always remember, a crawl is always better than never moving at all.

IMMANUEL

I'm not sure if I can handle the pressure.

> Our hope for you is unshaken, for we know that as you share in our sufferings, you will also share in our comfort. For we do not want you to be unaware, brothers, of the affliction we experienced in Asia. For we were so utterly burdened beyond our strength that we despaired of life itself. Indeed, we felt that we had received the sentence of death. But that was to make us rely not on ourselves but on God who raises the dead. (2 Corinthians 1:7–9, ESV)

Never be frightened when you are being faced with a trial. As a matter of fact, you should always be thankful because you know that you are on the fast track to an abundant life in Christ. Trials and tribulations are not to deter you away from God but rather to strengthen you. When you come to a trial in your life who will you trust? Will it be God who is all mighty, or yourself who is all vanity? Think about it.

> "They speak vanity every one with his neighbor: with flattering lips and a double heart do they speak." (Psalm 12: 2, NIV)

A great saying is this: "We have no right to ask God when sorrow comes, 'Why did this happen to me?' unless we ask the same question for every moment of happiness that comes our way" (author unknown).

How am I going to change my spirit? The answer is simple: it's in God's Word (the Holy Bible). The Bible was made as an instruction for your living. Why don't you take a look at some of the excuses that you might start giving on why not to read the Bible?

- I do not have a Bible, or I can't find my Bible.
- My kids need my attention, and God can wait.

- There is no time in my day; God will understand my busy schedule.
- Work is so demanding and is draining all my energy. When it calms down, I'll have time for God.
- My social life is a mess—I mean a *huge* mess—and I need to sort it out before I can spend time reading the Bible.
- I couldn't get the book.
- I'm really sick, and the doctor said I should sleep and not read the Bible.
- I am so tired. I just want to spend time on Twitter and play Facebook games, and not spend time with God.
- Seriously, me, read a Bible? The whole house would burn down, and my family would think I had a terminal illness.
- I've already read the Bible and got nothing out of it.
- I'm too young and won't have fun. When I'm old, I'll read it.
- There are so many translations; I don't know which one to get.
- I don't like books that you can't finish or read cover to cover.
- I'll be converted to a religion, waking up one day to discover I'm wearing WWJD shorts!
- Bible-speaking people are stern, serious, strict, and scary. They carry yellow notes with the word *guilt* on it and play tag with the other.
- I've heard bad things about the Bible, and we all know gossip is reliable information.
- I don't understand what I am reading. After all, the Bible was originally written in another language thousands of years ago.
- I like my current state of laziness, and God said I should take a daily rest.
- It's really boring, and I get much more inspiration from the popular books and television shows. Who needs scripture!
- There's nothing in it for me. Sinners don't own, read, or study the Bible.
- I'm too scared to face God.

What else can you put on this list? There is still room. Now that you covered every excuse that you could have not to read the Bible, let's take a look at what the scripture says about the Bible.

> For whatever things were written before were written for our learning, that we through the patience and comfort of the Scriptures might have hope. (Romans 15:4, NKJV)

> You search and investigate and pore over the Scriptures diligently, because you suppose and trust that you have eternal life through them. And these [very Scriptures] testify about Me! (John 5:39, AMP)

> You have been taught the holy Scriptures from childhood, and they have given you the wisdom to receive the salvation that comes by trusting in Christ Jesus. All Scripture is inspired by God and is useful to teach us what is true and to make us realize what is wrong in our lives. It corrects us when we are wrong and teaches us to do what is right. God uses it to prepare and equip his people to do every good work. (2 Timothy 3:15–17, NLT)

The Bible was written to prepare you for your good work. Notice the word *work*. You were not meant to read the Bible and keep it to yourself. You need to share the Word of God with everyone by your own actions and the way you speak. There are three phases you can take to help you understand the Word of God. By understanding what you are reading, the effects in your life will be greater than you can imagine possible. These three stages will help you learn in depth what God is trying to say to you as you read the Bible and be able to reflect it unto others like a mirror.

1. Read the Bible (Information Stage)
2. What is the scripture saying to me? (Analyzing Stage)
3. How can I put what I have learned to use today? (Sharing Stage)

Information Stage

The Information Stage is the gathering (processing) of information in any manner detectable by you. As such, it is a process that describes everything that is happening to you at that very moment. In this stage, your mind is gathering all the plausible information from the Bible.

Analyzing Stage

The Analyzing Stage is the process of examining what you read in great detail in order to understand the Bible better, or even discover more about it. In this stage, it takes a four-step breakdown.

1. You define all that you read in the Bible on that day.
2. You establish an understanding of what God is trying to say to you through the Bible.
3. You develop a plan of action on what God needs you to do through the Bible.
4. You decide whether or not you want to accept what God has planted in your heart through the Bible.

Sharing Stage

The Sharing Stage is the time to reveal to others the information that God has given you through the Bible. These are the calling of your own personal understanding of what you read in the Bible and sharing it with others. Your message will always be different from others because you are unique. Remember that the reason for the difference is you are reading Gods living Word and it will take your own past experiences to mold you into what God has created you for.

Body

> Do you not know that your body is the temple (the very sanctuary) of the Holy Spirit Who lives within you, Whom you have received [as a Gift] from God? You are not your own. (1 Corinthians 6:19, AMP)

Body is the physical groundwork or the foundation of your life. Now that your blueprint (soul) is starting to establish, you can begin to stabilize your foundation. In order for you to feel emotionally secure, your physical health plays a significant part of the transformation. This program is not here to generate a physical personality of vanity. That is far from it. It is intended to build your external persona of who you are and bring it to the surface. God created you in His image. It's now time for you to physically observe what God created in you.

This program will start to show you what a beautiful creation you are not only spiritually but also physically. When you look at yourself each day, you will begin to gradually see the change in your spirit as well as in your body. Here you will have a workout journal at the end of each day. There is a sample of the journal on the next page. Do not leave these pages blank. It will help you be accountable for what you have done for that day. It will be up to you to keep up with your own workout journal as well as your own meal plan that you will follow. There are many workout plans to choose from, so be sure you choose what is right for you. God took much time and pride in creating you just the way you are, perfect in every manner. Now it is time for you to take the moment to focus on your own personal workout program.

> The lamp of the body is the eye. If therefore your eye is good, your whole body will be full of light. But if your eye

is bad, your whole body will be full of darkness. If therefore the light that is in you is darkness, how great is that darkness! (Matthew 6:22–23, NKJV)

On the next page is the workout journal you will be filling in. Be sure to fill it in as much as possible so you can know your own progress in your workout.

L.E.A.P 27 Daily Workout Log

Date (Day/Month/Year): _____

Start Time: _____

End Time: _____

Scale Weight:	
Body Fat %:	
Fitness Goal:	Strength/Muscle Building/Fat Loss/Endurance/Other:

Body Parts Trained (Circle all that apply):

Whole Body | Chest | Back | Shoulders | Legs | Calves | Biceps | Triceps | Abs | Other: _____

CARDIO/AEROBIC/CONDITIONING EXERCISE

EXERCISE	TIME	DISTANCE/INTENSITY

WEIGHT, STRENGTH & RESISTANCE TRAINING

EXERCISE	WEIGHT	SETS	REPS	REST	NOTES

DIET & NUTRITION

MEAL	FOODS EATEN	APPROXIMATE CALORIES
BREAKFAST:		
LUNCH:		
DINNER:		

SELF EVALUATION

OVERALL WORKOUT RATING (1-10)		IMPROVEMENT NOTES:	

| 35 |

Mind

> A wise man is strong; yea, a man of knowledge increaseth strength. (Proverbs 24:5, KJV)

Mind is the final piece of the structure that is built, starting from the blueprint (soul) of your life, moving on to the foundation (body), which you will lay out. You must continue to add to the design of your structure every day by reading the Bible and studying more in depth the Word of the God. In this section, you will start by reading Romans, and at the end of each chapter, there will be a question-and-answer portion. Plus, you will sit and meditate for a couple of minutes a day on what you read. Meditation is an important factor that has truly been left out in this day and age. You live in a fast pace world with no time to just sit and meditate on God's word. God wants to speak to you, but how can you hear his voice if you don't learn the art of silence. This is a very simple and painless process that will expand your knowledge of what God has for you.

> Keep this Book of the Law always on your lips; meditate on it day and night, so that you may be careful to do everything written in it. Then you will be prosperous and successful. (Joshua 1:8, NIV)

During this portion, you will take a four-step process in order to answer the questions.

1. Read all the questions before reading the chapter. Familiarize yourself with what you are about to read.
2. There will be a verse number at the end of the question in which the answers will be found.
3. Read the entire chapter that is needed for the day.
4. Answer all the questions.

What makes this program so resilient is that there are two foundations that no one can ever take away from your life: your mind and soul, which can never be taken from you. Your body will eventually grow to become weak, but because of the strength of the other two, you are preparing a solid building for your life. In this section, your daily activity will focus on preparing your mind to become stronger and more knowledgeable.

> For this very reason, make every effort to add to your faith goodness; and to goodness, knowledge; and to knowledge, self-control; and to self-control, perseverance; and to perseverance, godliness; and to godliness, mutual affection; and to mutual affection, love. For if you possess these qualities in increasing measure, they will keep you from being ineffective and unproductive in your knowledge of our Lord Jesus Christ. (2 Peter 1:5–8, NIV)

This is a great outlook for your transformation. You will come to find out that when you complete the 27-day program, you will have an abundance of "love," which you will give "mutual affection" toward God and his children. Then you will "persevere" to gain "self-control" from the "knowledge" of your "goodness" in your "faith."

It is also equally important to journal your experiences throughout the day. Write about your day, or even what you learned for that day. When you write it, you can visually see the practices that you are performing during the next 27 days.

God didn't just speak to Moses about the Ten Commandments and then say "Go follow my words." God etched it in stone so no one could have any excuses if they had forgotten them. This is called accountability, and each journal entry will hold you accountable for your actions on that day. In this aspect, you too will write about your knowledge and journey so you can stay on track and gradually see the transformation from day 1 to day 27.

IMMANUEL

Finally, brethren, farewell (rejoice)! Be strengthened (perfected, completed, made what you ought to be); be encouraged and consoled and comforted; be of the same [agreeable] mind one with another; live in peace, and [then] the God of love [Who is the Source of affection, goodwill, love, and benevolence toward men] and the Author and Promoter of peace will be with you. (2 Corinthians 13:11, AMP)

After you read and answer the question, just take some time every day to meditate on what you read. Meditation takes a lot of practice in which you will train the mind or induce a mode of your personal consciousness, either to realize God's benefit in His Word or to just clear your mind of all problems the world will throw at you. Your own stress can make you feel hopeless, irritated, and upset. It can even affect your personal health. We all often think that we are too busy to take the time to stop and just meditate. But meditation can actually give you more time by making your mind stiller and more focused. Simple ten or fifteen minutes a day will help with your breathing and meditation practice. You will learn to overcome your stress level and find some inner peace and balance through Jesus Christ.

Meditation will also help you to understand your own mind. You can and will learn how to transform your mind from the negative effects of this world to positive insights on God's views, from disturbed to peaceful, from unhappy to happy. It all starts with meditating in Jesus Christ.

I will meditate on your precepts and fix my eyes on your ways, (Psalm 119:15, ESV)

I will also meditate on all Your work, And talk of Your deeds. (Psalm 77:12, NKJV)

Let the proud be ashamed, For they treated me wrongfully with falsehood; But I will meditate on Your precepts. (Psalm 119:78, NKJV)

O God, we meditate on your unfailing love as we worship in your Temple. (Psalm 48:9, NLT)

Are you discouraged yet? Like I said in the beginning, this is not your ordinary plan to change your personal life. We are going to the heart of it all: your Creator or Architect (God), your Contractor or Foreman (Jesus Christ), your blueprint (soul), your foundation (body), and, finally, your building structure (mind).

Now it is time to embark on a new beginning of happiness for the rest of your life. On the next page, there will be a written contract from the Word of the God. This is the ultimate commitment that you will make before God, so make sure you are ready to complete the next 27 days. On the contract, there are empty spaces where you will be entering your name. Once you have written your name on the contract and signed it, make sure you cut it out of the book and place it in a frame so you can remind yourself of this covenant between God and you.

Warning:

This is not for the fainthearted. This book is meant to challenge and commit you to go through a 27-day transformation of your only true existence and purpose of your life. I cannot express to you that this is a hard-hitting process that tests your soul, mind, and body vigorously. If you are ready, then you will sign the contract on the next page.

Where Is God?

When times are tough, who dismisses who,
Do you dismiss God, or does God dismiss you?
You have a hard life the first day you awake,
And you pray day by day in hopes you don't break.
The question in your mind can be answered by one,
It's the Alpha and Omega's only begotten Son.
The question you ask, "Where is God?"
Could He be that seed tucked away in a mother's pod,
Or could He be the air in which you breathe,
Or the knowledge that you conceive?
What about the wind that caresses your face
Or the diversity of souls in which you call race?
Could He be the water you consume every day?
Or the lakes that you swim in while the sun shines its rays?
Maybe God is not black or white, a she or he.
Maybe God's all around you, just maybe.
"Where is God?" you may ask from time to time.
God is everywhere, even hidden in this rhyme.

A Letter from Deceit

Hello. Just in case you forgot me, I am your deceit.

I hate this book you are about to read. I hate the concept of the whole mind, body, and soul, especially the soul portion of it. I hate this 27-day God-based program. To you who come in contact with me, I wish you suffering, and I wish you death. Allow me to introduce myself: I am the greatest trick in the world. I made you believe that I never even existed, and still continue to. I am cunning, baffling, and powerful. That's me. I have killed millions, and I am pleased with the outcome.

I love to catch you with the element of surprise. I love pretending I am your friend and lover. I have given you comfort, haven't I? Wasn't I there when you were lonely? When you wanted to die, didn't you call on me? I am your drug of choice. I come to your rescue when you need me. When you are hurting, I love to make you hurt even more. I love to make you cry. Better yet, I love to make you so numb where you can neither get hurt nor cry. When you can't feel anything at all, that's my true gratification. And all that I ask from you is long-term suffering. I've been there for you always, and I will be as long as you let me.

When things were going right in your life, you always invite me in. You said you didn't deserve these good things, and I was the only one who would agree with you. Together we were able to destroy all the good things in your life. People don't take me seriously. You fool. Without my help, these things would not be

IMMANUEL

possible. I am hated by you so much, and yet I do not come uninvited. You choose to have me over reality and peace.

More than you hate me, I hate all of you who have this LEAP 27 program. All of these things weaken me, and I can't function in the manner I am accustomed to. Now I must lie here quietly. You don't see me, but I am growing bigger than ever. When you only exist, I can live. When you live, I may only exist. But I am here, and I'm waiting. You are damaged and are extremely dangerous because I know you can survive without me.

Until we meet again—if we ever meet again—I wish you suffering and death.

Sincerely, your one true friend,
Deceit

Be sober, be vigilant; because your adversary the devil, as a roaring lion, walketh about, seeking whom he may devour: Whom resist steadfast in the faith, knowing that the same afflictions are accomplished in your brethren that are in the world. (1 Peter 5:8–9, KJV)

LEAP 27 Contract

"Therefore say to you _____, 'this is what the Sovereign Lord says: It is not for your sake, _____, that I am going to do these things, but for the sake of my holy name, which you have profaned among the nations where you have gone. I will show the holiness of my great name, which has been profaned among the nations, the name you have profaned among them. Then the nations will know that I am the Lord, declares the Sovereign Lord, when I am proved holy through you before their eyes. "'For I will take you out of the nations; I will gather you from all the countries and bring you back into your own land. I will sprinkle clean water on you, and you will be clean; I will cleanse you from all your impurities and from all your idols. I will give you a new heart and put a new spirit in you; I will remove from you your heart of stone and give you a heart of flesh. And I will put my Spirit in you and move you to follow my decrees and be careful to keep my laws. Then you will live in the land I gave your ancestors; you will be my people, and I will be your God. I will save you from all your uncleanness. I will call for the grain and make it plentiful and will not bring famine upon you. I will increase the fruit of the trees and the crops of the field, so that you will no longer suffer disgrace among the nations because of famine. Then you will remember your evil ways and wicked deeds, and you

IMMANUEL

will loathe yourselves for your sins and detestable practices. I want you to know that I am not doing this for your
sake, declares the Sovereign Lord. Be ashamed and dis-
graced for your conduct, _____!
(Ezekiel 36:22–32, NIV)

Day 1

FASTING/OLD YOU—
DESTROY YOUR TEMPLE

Daily Verse

He who covers his sins will not prosper, But whoever confesses and forsakes them will have mercy. (Proverbs 28:13, NKJV)

Put to death, therefore, whatever belongs to your earthly nature: sexual immorality, impurity, lust, evil desires and greed, which is idolatry. Because of these, the wrath of God is coming. You used to walk in these ways, in the life you once lived. But now you must also rid yourselves of all such things as these: anger, rage, malice, slander and filthy language from your lips. Do not lie to each other, since you have taken off your old self with its practices and have put on the new self, which is being renewed in knowledge in the image of its Creator. Here there is no Gentile or Jew, circumcised or uncircumcised, barbarian, Scythian, slave or free, but Christ is all, and is in all. Therefore, as God's chosen people, holy and dearly loved, clothe yourselves with compassion, kindness, humility, gentleness and patience. Bear with each other and forgive one another if any of you has a grievance against someone. Forgive as the Lord forgave you. And over all these virtues put on love, which binds them all together in perfect unity. Let the peace of Christ rule in your hearts, since as members of one body you were called to peace. And be thankful. Let the message of Christ dwell among you richly as you teach and admonish one another with all wisdom through psalms, hymns, and songs from the Spirit, singing to God with gratitude in your hearts. And whatever you do, whether in word or deed, do it all in the name of the Lord Jesus, giving thanks to God the Father through him. (Colossians 3:5–17, NIV)

Let's take a second to reflect on your old self. Don't hold anything back. Take a look deep into your heart, and ask these following questions:

- What has led me to my own pain and sorrow?
- Am I happy with where I am in my life?
- What can I do different to make my life so much easier?

God will show you that you are not as righteous as you think you are. None of us are, so don't feel like you're the only one. You are a sinner and have come short of the glory of God. God is not looking for your perfection; He is looking for your submission.

The fool says in his heart, "There is no God." They are corrupt, they do abominable deeds, there is none who does good. The Lord looks down from heaven on the children of man, to see if there are any who understand, who seek after God. They have all turned aside; together they have become corrupt; there is none who does good, not even one. (Psalms 14:1–3, ESV)

As it is written: "There is none righteous, no, not one; there is none who understands; There is none who seeks after God. They have all turned aside; They have together become unprofitable;

There is none who does good, no, not one." (Romans 3:10–12, NKJV)

"They rush to commit murder. Destruction and misery always follow them. They don't know where to find peace." "They have no fear of God at all." (Romans 3:15–18, NLT)

The way of peace they know not; and there is no judgment in their goings: they have made them crooked paths: whosoever goeth therein shall not know peace. (Isaiah 59:8, KJV)

Is that too bold of a statement for you to understand? Doesn't it hurt to read what God feels toward you on what you are doing and how wrong it is? Well, it should. This is called a conviction. The pain you are feeling is God the Father telling you that what you are doing is immoral. You may hide your sins from others, but the one presence that you can never hide sin from is God Almighty. People can read your words, but God reads your heart. What does your heart say and is it truly aligning with your words? God needs you to hold yourself accountable for your sins so you can have that special spiritual lifestyle. It is time for you to accept your own convictions and then mold them through Jesus Christ into contributions for others in life.

This is the day that you are going to destroy the old foundation that is in your life up to this point. In this part of the process don't try to rebuild what God is trying to destroy. There is a reason why God is destroying it so let it be. You will make an appointment to write in your journal all the things that you have done wrong in your life. So for today, you are going to go into overdrive. This is going to be the hardest part of the book: having to come to the realization that you are not worthy to receive God's one perfect gift. And that gift is the grace and love of his Son, Jesus Christ. Always remember that Jesus Christ came on to this earth for a purpose. He died on the cross for your sins, so why are you not confessing your sins to him? When you hold back, you are making what your Savior did for you an action done in vain. So just confess it and be saved. Jesus will turn your convictions to be God's grace. Jesus will turn your failures to be God's successes. Jesus will turn your defeat to be God's victory. Jesus will turn your history to be God's legacy. Jesus will turn your destiny to be God's memory. In return God will turn your death to be Jesus's resurrection.

> "All things have been committed to me by my Father. No one knows who the Son is except the Father, and no one knows who the Father is except the Son and those to whom the Son chooses to reveal him." (Luke 10:23, NIV)

> Therefore do not be ashamed of the testimony of our Lord, nor of me His prisoner, but share with me in the sufferings for the gospel according to the power of God, who has saved us and called us with a holy calling, not according to our works, but according to His own purpose and grace which was given to us in Christ Jesus before time began, but has now been revealed by the appearing of our Savior Jesus Christ, who has abolished death and brought life and immortality to light through the gospel. (2 Timothy 1:8–10, NKJV)

Today you are going to start fasting in order to discover the old you. For example, if you were to give up food just for today, the hunger pains remind you that you're hungry. Instead of eating to fill your physical pain, you will substitute with time to write in your journal, meditate on God's Word (Bible), pray, or think of all the things in your life that have caused you so much pain. This is called feeding your soul, and it's time to have a buffet. During these opportunities, you will be given a chance to become closer to God, who is the architect of your life.

> For he was [waiting expectantly and confidently] looking forward to the city which has fixed and firm foundations, whose Architect and Builder is God. (Hebrews 11:10, AMP)

How can fasting bring me closer to God? Fasting is the first line of defense on becoming closer to God. It's making a sacrifice for God in order to become closer to him. Here are some factors you must take when fasting.

1. When you begin to fast, make sure that it is done with the right motive, which is glorifying God and can be pleasing in his sight.

> "Why have we fasted," they say, "and you have not seen? Why have we afflicted our souls, and you take no notice?" In fact, in the day of your fast you find pleasure, and exploit all your laborers. Indeed you fast for strife and debate, and to strike with the fist of wickedness.
>
> You will not fast as you do this day, to make your voice heard on high. Is it a fast that I have chosen, a day for a man to afflict his soul? Is it to bow down his head like a bulrush, and to spread out sackcloth and ashes? Would you call this a fast, and an acceptable day to the Lord? "Is this not the fast that I have chosen: To loose the bonds of wickedness, to undo the heavy burdens, to let the oppressed go free, and that you break every yoke? Is it not to share your bread with the hungry, and that you bring to your house the poor who are cast out; when you see the naked, that you cover him, and not hide yourself from your own flesh? Then your light shall break forth like the morning, your

IMMANUEL

healing shall spring forth speedily, and your righteousness shall go before you; the glory of the Lord shall be your rear guard. Then you shall call, and the Lord will answer; you shall cry, and He will say, 'Here I am.' "If you take away the yoke from your midst, the pointing of the finger, and speaking wickedness, If you extend your soul to the hungry and satisfy the afflicted soul, Then your light shall dawn in the darkness, and your darkness shall be as the noonday. The Lord will guide you continually, and satisfy your soul in drought, and strengthen your bones; you shall be like a watered garden, and like a spring of water, whose waters do not fail. Those from among you shall build the old waste places; you shall raise up the foundations of many generations; and you shall be called the Repairer of the Breach, The Restorer of Streets to Dwell In. (Isaiah 58:3–12, NKJV)

2. Now when you fast, link yourself closely in prayer and reading the Bible, not just this book. Here you will feel the true meaning of your own transgressions in your life. This is the time to confess all your sins to Jesus Christ. Let the Christ of your life show you the true manner of your existence in life, which your sin has hidden from you.

Then I set my face toward the Lord God to make request by prayer and supplications, with fasting, sackcloth, and ashes. And I prayed to the Lord my God, and made confession, and said, "O Lord, great and awesome God, who keeps His covenant and mercy with those who love Him, and with those who keep His commandments, we have sinned and committed iniquity, we have done wickedly and rebelled, even by departing from Your precepts and Your judgments. Neither have we heeded Your servants the prophets, who spoke in Your name to our kings and our princes, to our fathers and all the people of the land.

O Lord, righteousness belongs to You, but to us shame of face, as it is this day—to the men of Judah, to the inhabitants of Jerusalem and all Israel, those near and those far off in all the countries to which You have driven them, because of the unfaithfulness which they have committed against You. "O Lord, to us belongs shame of face, to our kings, our princes, and our fathers, because we have sinned against You. To the Lord our God belong mercy and forgiveness, though we have rebelled against Him. We have not obeyed the voice of the Lord our God, to walk in His laws, which He set before us by His servants the prophets. Yes, all Israel has transgressed Your law, and has departed so as not to obey Your voice; therefore the curse and the oath written in the Law of Moses the servant of God have been poured out on us, because we have sinned against Him. (Daniel 9:3–11, NKJV)

3. The final key to fasting is that it is to be done in a manner of humility and secrecy. Do not let everyone know what you are doing. This is your time to be with Jesus, and you don't need to share what's going on with you today. You will have plenty of time to share many experiences about what God has done for you, but this is not one of them.

And when you fast, do not look gloomy like the hypocrites, for they disfigure their faces that their fasting may be seen by others. Truly, I say to you, they have received their reward. But when you fast, anoint your head and wash your face, that your fasting may not be seen by others but by your Father who is in secret. And your Father who sees in secret will reward you. (Matthew 6:16–18, ESV)

Jesus was tempted, and yet he overcame his temptation with the Word of God. The Bible is your ultimate tool that you will use to overcome any temptation in your life. Take the daily verses that

IMMANUEL

are provided for you at the beginning of each day so you can read and keep them with you. When you feel tempted, discouraged, or just feel alone, God doesn't want your best to try to overcome the temptation. Your best will always come with limitations. God wants you to submit to him so he can have the opportunity to do his best which is limitless, so open up that scripture and read it to yourself over and over. Always remember you are not alone, so stop isolating yourself. God is alive in his scriptures and is always with you. If you don't believe that, just try it.

> Then Jesus was led by the Spirit into the wilderness to be tempted by the devil. After fasting forty days and forty nights, he was hungry. The tempter came to him and said, "If you are the Son of God, tell these stones to become bread." Jesus answered, "It is written: 'Man shall not live on bread alone, but on every word that comes from the mouth of God.' Then the devil took him to the holy city and had him stand on the highest point of the temple. "If you are the Son of God," he said, "throw yourself down. For it is written: "'He will command his angels concerning you, and they will lift you up in their hand so that you will not strike your foot against a stone.'" Jesus answered him, "It is also written: 'Do not put the Lord your God to the test.'" Again, the devil took him to a very high mountain and showed him all the kingdoms of the world and their splendor. "All this I will give you," he said, "if you will bow down and worship me." Jesus said to him, "Away from me, Satan! For it is written: 'Worship the Lord your God, and serve him only.'" Then the devil left him, and angels came and attended him. (Matthew 4:1–11, NIV)

Don't take advantage of the poor just because you can; don't take advantage of those who stand helpless in court. The Lord will argue their case for them and threaten the life of anyone who threatens theirs. (Proverbs 22: 24-25)

LEAP Challenge

Your list for today is very important for your transformation of your personal life. Today when you make your list of the old you, be sure to include these subjects in your list:

- Sexual immorality
- Impurity
- Inappropriate behavior
- Idolatry
- Witchcraft
- Drug abuse
- Hatred
- Conflict toward others
- Fits of rage
- Dissensions
- Factions
- Envy
- Drunkenness

This is your own personal list. Do not cut yourself short from the grace of God. This is an acknowledgment that you are not perfect, but you have a perfect Savior waiting to forgive you. Don't let your excuses about your life circumstances being beyond your control be a way to rationalize a way to give up. The truth is that in every problem that life gives you always contain a seed to its own solution, so today plant that seed and watch the solution grow into improvement in your life.

L.E.A.P. Insight

As you go through today's challenge consider this, the devil can never create your future. He can only use your past to make you walk with him towards his future.

IMMANUEL

Mind

Romans Chapter 1

1. _____ was a servant of Christ and chosen by God to preach his Word. (1)

2. Paul has been trying to do what? (13)

> After these things were ended, Paul purposed in the spirit, when he had passed through Macedonia and Achaia, to go to Jerusalem, saying, After I have been there, I must also see Rome. (Acts 19:21, KJV)

3. What is Paul not ashamed of? (16)

> Whosoever therefore shall be ashamed of me and of my words in this adulterous and sinful generation; of him also shall the Son of man be ashamed, when he cometh in the glory of his Father with the holy angels. (Mark 8:8, KJV)

4. How does God put people right with themselves? (17)

> God also bearing witness both with signs and wonders, with various miracles, and gifts of the Holy Spirit, according to His own will? (Hebrews 2:4, NKJV)

5. Why doesn't mankind give God the honor? (21)

> Now this I say and testify in the Lord, that you must no longer walk as the Gentiles do, in the futility of their minds. They are darkened in their understanding, alienated from the life of God because of the ignorance that is in them, due to their hardness of heart. (Ephesians 4:17–18, ESV)

6. What does mankind choose to worship? (23)

> Lest you act corruptly and make for yourselves a carved image in the form of any figure: the likeness of male or female, the likeness of any animal that is on the earth or the likeness of any winged bird that flies in the air, the likeness of anything that creeps on the ground or the likeness of any fish that is in the water beneath the earth. (Deuteronomy 4:16–18, NKJV)

Mind Meditation Checklist

10 Minutes

> Praise to the God of All Comfort] Praise be to the God and Father of our Lord Jesus Christ, the Father of compassion and the God of all comfort, who comforts us in all our troubles, so that we can comfort those in any trouble with the comfort we ourselves receive from God. (2 Corinthians 1:3–4, NIV)

- Find a quiet comfortable place. Sit in a chair or on the floor with your head, neck, and back straight, but not stiff.
- Put aside all thoughts of the past and the future, and stay in the present. Focus on the verse above.
- Become aware of your breathing. With every breath you take, allow your body to be filled with the Holy Spirit.
- Scan your body, starting with your feet, and work your way up, always ending with your head.
- Focus on the sensation of air moving in and out of your body as you breathe.
- Release all your sin as you exhale, and invite all of God's Spirit as you inhale.
- Pay attention to the way each breath changes and is different.

IMMANUEL

- Watch every thought of sin, worry, fear, anxiety, or hate come into your mind, and release it with every exhale.
- When any thoughts come up in your mind, don't ignore or suppress them but simply observe them, remaining calm and collected, giving them all to the Lord.
- If you find yourself getting carried away in your thoughts, just focus back on Jesus, and simply return to your breathing, inhaling the Holy Spirit with every breath.
- Remember, do not be hard on yourself when you lose focus. You are just beginning a pure form of godly meditation.
- Now as the time comes to a close, sit for a minute or two, becoming aware of where you are, and get up gradually.

L.E.A.P. 27

Body

L.E.A.P 27 Daily Workout Log

Date (Day/Month/Year): _____

Start Time: _____

End Time: _____

Scale Weight:	
Body Fat %:	
Fitness Goal:	Strength/Muscle Building/Fat Loss/Endurance/Other:

Body Parts Trained (Circle all that apply):

Whole Body | Chest | Back | Shoulders | Legs | Calves | Biceps | Triceps | Abs | Other: _____

CARDIO/AEROBIC/CONDITIONING EXERCISE

EXERCISE	TIME	DISTANCE/INTENSITY

WEIGHT, STRENGTH & RESISTANCE TRAINING

EXERCISE	WEIGHT	SETS	REPS	REST	NOTES

DIET & NUTRITION

MEAL	FOODS EATEN	APPROXIMATE CALORIES
BREAKFAST:		
LUNCH:		
DINNER:		

SELF EVALUATION

OVERALL WORKOUT RATING (1-10)		IMPROVEMENT NOTES:	

Day 2

BUILDING THE NEW YOU

Daily Verse

And it shall come to pass, that whosoever shall call on the name of the Lord shall be saved. (Acts 2:21, KJV)

Blessed is he whose transgressions are forgiven, whose sins are covered. Blessed is the man whose sin the Lord does not count against him and in whose spirit is no deceit. When I kept silent, my bones wasted away through my groaning all day long. For day and night your hand was heavy upon me; my strength was sapped as in the heat of summer. Then I acknowledged my sin to you and did not cover up my iniquity. I said, "I will confess my transgressions to the Lord" and you forgave the guilt of my sin. Therefore let everyone who is godly pray to you while you may be found; surely when the mighty waters rise, they will not reach him. You are my hiding place; you will protect me from trouble and surround me with songs of deliverance. I will instruct you and teach you in the way you should go; I will counsel you and watch over you. Do not be like the horse or the mule, which have no understanding but must be controlled by bit and bridle or they will

IMMANUEL

not come to you. Many are the woes of the wicked, but
the Lord's unfailing love surrounds the man who trusts in
him. Rejoice in the Lord and be glad, you righteous; sing,
all you who are upright in heart! (Psalm 32, NIV)

Today will be the start of your new life, a start of a new beginning
toward your one true calling.

"Whatever happened yesterday, or whatever happens tomorrow, doesn't mean a thing for today" (author unknown).

Take a moment to look back at your list of the old you that
you wrote yesterday. Read the items to yourself, and meditate
on them, letting them make a substantial impact on your heart.
Don't focus on your big items on your list that caused you to fail,
but realize it's the little ones that built up over time and turned
you away from God. This is called the "Slow Fade Effect." This
process makes you emphasize on the big disappointments and
makes you forget about all the little fiascos that got you there.
Your list will reveal to you who you used to be and who you never
want to be again. Allow this old-you list to open your eyes to a
person who led you to a life of pain and suffering, a life that was
shackled and bonded by the complications of the world views.
But God always gives you a way out.

For God so greatly loved and dearly prized the world that
He [even] gave up His only begotten (unique) Son, so that
whoever believes in (trusts in, clings to, relies on) Him
shall not perish (come to destruction, be lost) but have
eternal (everlasting) life. For God did not send the Son
into the world in order to judge (to reject, to condemn, to
pass sentence on) the world, but that the world might find
salvation and be made safe and sound through Him. (John
3:16–17, AMP)

True love is what God has for you, and it is all in God's Word.
The above verse is such a boundless statement. God sent his only

begotten Son, Jesus, to die on the cross for *your* sins. Reread that sentence, and understand that Jesus was perfect in all ways. To every wrong person you will come to realize you mean nothing, but to the right person you will mean everything continually. You are and will always be the right person in Jesus's eyes. That's why he gave his life for you. He gave everything for your freedom, not because he had to, but because he loved you so much that he chose to. He was a sinless man who did nothing wrong, performed many miracles, and healed many people, the Son of God who took your place on the cross for all of your evil ways that you have written on that list.

> But God has now brought you to life with Christ. God forgave us all our sins; he canceled the unfavorable record of our debts with its binding rules and did away with it completely by nailing it to the cross. And on that cross Christ freed himself from the power of the spiritual rulers and authorities; he made a public spectacle of them by leading them as captives in his victory procession. (Colossians 2:13–15, NIV)

Your old list is no more. You are no longer bound and restrained by any of your sins in life. It is time to let go of the past, which lies in the list that you are holding on to in your hand. For all of us, this is a hard concept to grasp and understand. We take all our wrongdoings and hold on to them tight and don't want to let go of them. This list of sin is what has corrupted your life into believing you are not created for something more, but God says you are. You are like a rose to God which is very lovely at sight. There is never an unpleasant rose to the eyes. While a rose is growing in the roots they develop very painful thorns on their stems. No matter how many thorns are on the rose it's the pure essence of the flower itself that blossoms with sheer elegance. It's not until the florists gets a hold of the rose and clips its thorns completely off that the rose becomes a perfect flower. It is gorgeous in sight, easy to handle and becomes such a great gift to give. Even though it hurts the rose to clip the thorns, the stems itself begin to callus over. The thorns never grow back no matter what. In this sense God is your personal florist, you are the beautiful rose, and the thorns themselves are that list you are holding. God is clipping away at your very core to make you a perfect gift for others to enjoy. You are truly forgiven of your list. Don't let anyone tell you that you are not forgiven, when God says you are. This is an opportunity that was given to you: a second chance at a new beginning in your life. You have to just give up all of your sins to Christ Jesus.

> He who covers his sins will not prosper, But whoever confesses and forsakes them will have mercy. (Proverbs 28:13, NKJV)

You have been given a wonderful gift toward that new beginning, and that gift is forgiveness. This gift cannot be bought, just received into your heart. God has given you the greatest gift, yet you are trying to pay him back in some way. God doesn't want your money; he wants your love and faith to believe in his Son, your Savior, Jesus Christ, who died on the cross for your sins. You are forgiven, and that is that. Learn to accept this gift that God has given you.

Now close your eyes and say a prayer. Ask Jesus for forgiveness of all your sins that you have written on paper. Also, you need to ask him to come into your heart. You need to use your own words when you pray this prayer. The reason is so simple: Jesus truly knows what is in your heart, and now he wants you to confess your sins with all your heart.

> Because, if you confess with your mouth that Jesus is Lord and believe in your heart that God raised him from the dead, you will be saved. For with the heart one believes and is justified, and with the mouth one confesses and is saved. (Romans 10:9–10, ESV)

You are putting your sins up on the cross where Jesus shed his blood. You have to understand that as Christ was beaten and bruised, it was by your sin that allowed this to happen. It was by your sin that our Savior was destroyed. This was the purpose of Jesus's one calling. Never let his purpose be taken in vain.

> Then they struck Him on the head with a reed and spat on Him; and bowing the knee, they worshiped Him. And when they had mocked Him, they took the purple off Him, put His own clothes on Him, and led Him out to crucify Him. (Mark 15:19–20, NKJV)

It is by your sin that the cross was carried to Golgotha (the Place of the Skull). But notice that Jesus didn't carry the cross. A man named Simon was forced to carry the cross. This is important, because your sin is that cross. It is a heavy burden that you are dragging. That is the true representation of the cross. The cross was a form of execution back in those days. It was as evil as the death chamber or the electric chair. That is what you sin represents. So as Simon carried the cross, you have carried your cross (sin) long enough.

> And as they led him away, they laid hold upon one Simon, a Cyrenian, coming out of the country, and on him they laid the cross, that he might bear it after Jesus. (Luke 23:26, KJV)

Notice how Simon carried the cross and Jesus was in front of him. Jesus led the way to redemption. It is by your sin that Christ was pierced with nails and crucified. You carried the cross (sin), and Jesus gave his life on it in order to wash you clean of your filth.

> And when they crucified Him, they divided His garments, casting lots for them to determine what every man should take. (Mark 15:24, NKJV)

IMMANUEL

And it is by Jesus Christ, who was lifted from the grave and resurrected so he could defeat sin, which would lead you to death. Your sins have been lifted with Christ and brought to the Father as his Son represents you.

> And he said to them, "Do not be alarmed. You seek Jesus of Nazareth, who was crucified. He has risen; he is not here. See the place where they laid him. (Mark 16:6, ESV)

And now that Christ is representing you as he pleads with the Father to send you the greatest gift: a renewed soul and a release from the bondage of sin, which is death. He is preparing your body to receive the Holy Spirit, who will guide you in your spiritual walk. Later, you will learn more about the Holy Spirit.

> "And now I will send the Holy Spirit, just as my Father promised. But stay here in the city until the Holy Spirit comes and fills you with power from heaven." (Luke 24:49, NLT)

Don't make friends with people who have hot, violent tempers. You might learn their habits and not be able to change. (Proverbs 22: 26–27)

LEAP Challenge 2

Today you are going to write out a new-you list. In this list, include the following factors:

- What future are you looking for?
- List some short-term goals for the next 27 days.
- What do you want to accomplish emotionally during the next 27 days?
- How do you want to act?
- List the positive emotions that you want to have in your life.

L.E.A.P. 27

After you have completed your new-you list, compare the two lists. Try to visualize what you need to do to go from the old you and move onward toward the new you. Now when that is done, I want you to grab your old-you list and throw it away. This is a new bold statement that you will make to yourself that your old self is on that cross with Jesus. You are no longer bound or shackled by sin. You are now free from the tyranny of sin and ready to start a new life in Christ, who forgave you and washed away all your sins. Now you have to let go of your past and just throw it away. Here is a great example of how forgiveness works:

When one of the Pharisees invited Jesus to have dinner with him, he went to the Pharisee's house and reclined at the table. A woman in that town who lived a sinful life learned that Jesus was eating at the Pharisee's house, so she came there with an alabaster jar of perfume. As she stood behind him at his feet weeping, she began to wet his feet with her tears. Then she wiped them with her hair, kissed them and poured perfume on them. When the Pharisee who had invited him saw this, he said to himself, "If this man were a prophet, he would know who is touching him and what kind of woman she is—that she is a sinner." Jesus answered him, "Simon, I have something to tell you." "Tell me, teacher," he said. "Two people owed money to a certain moneylender. One owed him five hundred denarii, and the other fifty. Neither of them had the money to pay him back, so he forgave the debts of both. Now which of them will love him more?" Simon replied, "I suppose the one who had the bigger debt forgiven." "You have judged correctly," Jesus said. Then he turned toward the woman and said to Simon, "Do you see this woman? I came into your house. You did not give me any water for my feet, but she wet my feet with her tears and wiped them with her hair. You did not give me a kiss, but this woman, from the time I entered, has not stopped kissing my feet. You did

IMMANUEL

not put oil on my head, but she has poured perfume on my feet. Therefore, I tell you, her many sins have been forgiven—as her great love has shown. But whoever has been forgiven little loves little." Then Jesus said to her, "Your sins are forgiven." The other guests began to say among themselves, "Who is this who even forgives sins?" Jesus said to the woman, "Your faith has saved you; go in peace." (Luke 7:36–50, NIV)

L.E.A.P. Insight

Once you are done with the new you list, write yourself a letter that you can pull out and read every day from this point on. Start by saying, "Dear Lord Jesus, Please make my love patient, my love kind. I don't want to envy, I don't want to boast, and I don't want to be proud. I don't want my love to dishonor others, I don't want to be self-seeking, I don't want to be easily angered, I don't want my love to keep any record of wrongs. My love does not delight in evil but rejoices with your truth. I want my love to always protect, always trust, always hope, and always persevere. I never want my love to fail. Amen.

Mind

Romans Chapter 2

1. What happens when you judge others? (1)

   Judge not, that you be not judged. (Matthew 7:1, NKJV)

   Judge not, and you shall not be judged. Condemn not, and you shall not be condemned. Forgive, and you will be forgiven. (Luke 6:37, NKJV)

L.E.A.P. 27

2. According to what you have done what will God do for you? (6)

> God has spoken once, twice have I heard this: that power belongs to God. Also to You, O Lord, belong mercy and loving–kindness, for You render to every man according to his work. (Psalms 62:11–12, AMP)

> If you [profess ignorance and] say, Behold, we did not know this, does not He Who weighs and ponders the heart perceive and consider it? And He Who guards your life, does not He know it? And shall not He render to [you and] every man according to his works? (Proverbs 24:12, AMP)

3. T or F_____ God does not judge everyone by the same standards. (11)

> For the Lord your God is God of gods and Lord of lords, the great God, mighty and awesome, who shows no partiality nor takes a bribe. (Deuteronomy 10:17, NKJV)

4. T or F_____ The Gentiles always spoke evil of God. (24)

> Now therefore, what have I here," says the Lord, "That My people are taken away for nothing?
> Those who rule over them make them wail," says the Lord, "And My name is blasphemed continually every day. (Isaiah 52:5, NKJV)

IMMANUEL

Mind Meditation Checklist

10 Minutes

> Strip yourselves of your former nature [put off and discard your old unrenewed self] which characterized your previous manner of life and becomes corrupt through lusts and desires that spring from delusion; And be constantly renewed in the spirit of your mind [having a fresh mental and spiritual attitude], and put on the new nature (the regenerate self) created in God's image, [Godlike] in true righteousness and holiness. (Ephesians 4:22–24, AMP)

- Find a quiet comfortable place. Sit in a chair or on the floor with your head, neck and back straight, but not stiff.
- Put aside all thoughts of the past and the future and stay in the present. Focus on the verse above.
- Become aware of your breathing. With every breath you take, allow your body to be filled with the Holy Spirit.
- Scan your body, starting with your feet, and work your way up, always ending with your head.
- Focus on the sensation of air moving in and out of your body as you breathe.
- Release all your sin as you exhale, and invite all of God's Spirit as you inhale.
- Pay attention to the way each breath changes and is different.
- Watch every thought of sin, worry, fear, anxiety, or hate come into your mind, and release it with every exhale.
- When any thoughts come up in your mind, don't ignore or suppress them but simply observe them, remaining calm and collected, giving them all to the Lord.
- If you find yourself getting carried away in your thoughts, just focus back on Jesus and simply return to your breathing, inhaling the Holy Spirit with every breath.

L.E.A.P. 27

- Remember, do not be hard on yourself when you lose focus. You are just beginning a pure form of godly meditation.
- Now as the time comes to a close, sit for a minute or two, becoming aware of where you are, and get up gradually.

Body

L.E.A.P 27 Daily Workout Log

Date (Day/Month/Year): _____

Start Time: _____

End Time: _____

Scale Weight:	
Body Fat %:	
Fitness Goal:	Strength/Muscle Building/Fat Loss/Endurance/Other:

Body Parts Trained (Circle all that apply):

Whole Body | Chest | Back | Shoulders | Legs | Calves | Biceps | Triceps | Abs | Other: _____

CARDIO/AEROBIC/CONDITIONING EXERCISE

EXERCISE	TIME	DISTANCE/INTENSITY

WEIGHT, STRENGTH & RESISTANCE TRAINING

EXERCISE	WEIGHT	SETS	REPS	REST	NOTES

DIET & NUTRITION

MEAL	FOODS EATEN	APPROXIMATE CALORIES
BREAKFAST:		
LUNCH:		
DINNER:		

SELF EVALUATION

OVERALL WORKOUT RATING (1-10)		IMPROVEMENT NOTES:	

Day 3

LOVE EVERYONE

Daily Verse

You have heard that it was said, "You shall love your neighbor and hate your enemy." But I say to you, love your enemies, bless those who curse you, do good to those who hate you, and pray for those who spitefully use you and persecute you. (Matthew 5:43–44, NKJV)

And now I will show you the most excellent way. If I speak in the tongues of men and of angels, but have not love, I am only a resounding gong or a clanging cymbal. If I have the gift of prophecy and can fathom all mysteries and all knowledge, and if I have a faith that can move mountains, but have not love, I am nothing. If I give all I possess to the poor and surrender my body to the flames, but have not love, I gain nothing. Love is patient, love is kind. It does not envy, it does not boast, it is not proud. It is not rude, it is not self-seeking, it is not easily angered, and it keeps no record of wrongs. Love does not delight in evil but rejoices with the truth. It always protects, always trusts, always hopes, and always perseveres. Love never fails. But where there are prophecies, they will cease; where there are tongues, they will be stilled; where there is knowledge, it will pass away. For we know in part and we prophesy in part, but when perfection comes, the imperfect disappears. When I was a child, I talked like a child, I thought like a child, I reasoned like a child. When I became a man, I put childish ways behind me. Now we see but a poor reflection as in a mirror; then we shall see face to face. Now I know in part; then I shall know fully, even as I am known. And now these three remain: faith, hope and love. But the greatest of these is love. (1 Corinthians 13, NIV)

Love is the basis of your new foundation. Every day you will say to yourself, "Love everyone, enjoy every moment, accept any situation, and praise God." This is a very important part of your transformation. Today, "Love everyone" is your main focus. I know what you're thinking.

- Why should you love everyone?
- Have you seen the world out there?
- Or better yet, how do we love everyone?

How do we love people who lie, cheat, steal, kill, live in hate; people who cause physical and emotional abuse—this list can go on and on, but let's put it into God's perspective and how he views love.

For God so loved the world that He gave His only begotten Son, that whoever believes in Him should not perish but have everlasting life. (John 3:16, NKJV)

Here you learn that no matter how bad your sins, God loved you so dearly that he sent his only Son to wash away your iniquity. If you read a little further to John 3:17 he also states that he didn't send his Son into this world to condemn us, but to save us.

Now God is showing you how much he loves you. God's love in this above passage was not a word, but the process he had to do in order to stay active in your life so he can perform the act of grace. Let's take a look at how much the Son loves you as well.

> We know what real love is because Jesus gave up his life for us. So we also ought to give up our lives for our brothers and sisters. (1 John 3:16, NLT)

Now in this passage, you can clearly see that Jesus Christ showed us how to love just as well. He laid down his life for you, the sinner. Jesus was sent to cleanse all your sins, but don't forget, Christ was a spiritual man who had faith in the Father and had the same emotions as you. He was tempted by the same temptations of the world, yet he still loved us so much that he never faltered toward sin. Christ conquered it. Jesus became the "surrender agreement" to the Father and the "destruction agreement" to sin, which you desire so dearly, all for the sake of your demise so you could be considered by the Father to having a higher, more pressing purpose in his eyes. God presented the act of grace, while Jesus revealed the obedience of grace.

In today's culture, love is defined in three categories.

1. Feel tender affection for somebody, such as a close relative or friend, or for something, such as a place, an ideal, or an animal.
2. Feel desire for somebody: to feel romantic and sexual desire and longing for somebody.
3. Like something very much: to like something, or like doing something very much.

Now above, you can truly see that the devil has turned love into a feeling and liking. The three descriptions are how you would try to label the word *love*. Love was never meant to be contained by just a word or label; instead it was supposed to be an action. The

IMMANUEL

world (devil) tells you to choose which depiction of the term love best suits the occasion you're in, but God never intended for this to just be a simple word. Love was and will always be an action, a one true act, and a deed of utter significance for one another and once you learn how to live by it you will never be the same.

> Dear friends, let us love one another, for love comes from God. Everyone who loves has been born of God and knows God. Whoever does not love does not know God, because God is love. This is how God showed his love among us: He sent his one and only Son into the world that we might live through him. This is love: not that we loved God, but that he loved us and sent his Son as an atoning sacrifice for our sins. Dear friends, since God so loved us, we also ought to love one another. No one has ever seen God; but if we love one another, God lives in us and his love is made complete in us. This is how we know that we live in him and he in us: He has given us of his Spirit. And we have seen and testify that the Father has sent his Son to be the Savior of the world. If anyone acknowledges that Jesus is the Son of God, God lives in them and they in God. And so we know and rely on the love God has for us. God is love. Whoever lives in love lives in God, and God in them. This is how love is made complete among us so that we will have confidence on the Day of Judgment: In this world we are like Jesus. There is no fear in love. But perfect love drives out fear, because fear has to do with punishment. The one who fears is not made perfect in love. We love because he first loved us. Whoever claims to love God yet hates a brother or sister is a liar. For whoever does not love their brother and sister, whom they have seen, cannot love God, whom they have not seen. And he has given us this command: Anyone who loves God must also love their brother and sister. (1 John 4:7–21, NIV)

How can you know God if you don't know how to love? Or better yet, how can you believe that there is a God at all if you truly have never experienced his love that he intended for you to have?

> For the law was given by Moses, but grace and truth came by Jesus Christ. No man hath seen God at any time, the only begotten Son, which is in the bosom of the Father, he hath declared him. (John 1:17–18, KJV)

Jesus was sent to show you how to love and lead the way. God created love as an action, and it was the devil who defined it. You are now living the *definition* of love and not the *action* of love, the way that it was intended. You see, the devil defined love and turned it into his own word. Take a look at it for yourself; look at how many different ways love can be changed.

Of course you haven't seen God, because God is love and Jesus was the representation of God to teach you how to love. If you don't have Christ in your heart, can you truly learn how to love?

> And he said to him, "You shall love the Lord your God with all your heart and with all your soul and with all your mind. This is the great and first commandment. And a second is like it: You shall love your neighbor as yourself. On these two commandments depend all the Law and the Prophets." (Matthew 22:37–40, ESV)

To know the true power of love and meaning it all starts with Jesus Christ. He made it very clear if we love our God and love our neighbor, then all other commandments would fall into play. It is time for you to start to love one another in Jesus Christ name.

> For the commandments, "You shall not commit adultery," "You shall not murder," "You shall not steal," "You shall not bear false witness," "You shall not covet," and if there is any

other commandment, are all summed up in this saying, namely, "You shall love your neighbor as yourself." Love does no harm to a neighbor; therefore love is the fulfillment of the law. (Romans 13:9–10, NKJV)

Don't promise to be responsible for someone else's debts. If you should be unable to pay, they will take away even your bed. (Proverbs 22: 28)

Love everyone.

LEAP Challenge 3

Share the love that you have in your heart, whether it be with family, friends, or even a complete stranger. There are many ways to show your love. The advice for today is "Love everybody." Your challenge for today will be to keep your own tracking list on which person you showed love to on this glorious day. Don't be afraid to love. Just embrace it.

L.E.A.P. Insight

Go to a beloved person today and express to them how much you truly love them. Then sit back and take a look at the reaction that they give to you. It is in their response you will find that love has always and forever had an identity.

Mind

Romans Chapter 3

1. God must be _____, even though every man is a liar. (4)

> Against You, You only, have I sinned, and done this evil in Your sight—That You may be found just when You speak, and blameless when You judge. (Psalms 51:4, NKJV)

L.E.A.P. 27

2. T or F _____ We all are righteous in the sight of God. (10)

> They have all turned aside; together they have become corrupt; there is none who does good, not even one. (Psalms 14:3, ESV)

> Every one of them is gone back: they are altogether become filthy; there is none that doeth good, no, not one. (Psalms 53:3, KJV)

3. Their _____ are open graves; their _____ practice deceit. (13)

> For there is no faithfulness in their mouth; Their inward part is destruction; Their throat is an open tomb; They flatter with their tongue. (Psalms 5:9, NKJV)

> They have sharpened their tongues like a serpent; adders' poison is under their lips. (Psalms 140:3, KJV)

4. Their _____ are full of cursing and bitterness. (14)

> His mouth is full of cursing and deceit and fraud: under his tongue is mischief and vanity. (Psalms 10:7, KJV)

5. T or F _____ The way of peace they do not know. (17)

> Their feet run to evil, And they make haste to shed innocent blood;
>   Their thoughts are thoughts of iniquity; Wasting and destruction are in their paths. The way of peace they have not known, And there is no justice in their ways; They have made themselves crooked paths; Whoever takes that way shall not know peace. (Isaiah 59:7–8, NKJV)

| 79 |

IMMANUEL

6. There is no _____ of God before their eyes. (18)

   Sin whispers to the wicked, deep within their hearts. They have no fear of God at all. (Psalm 36: 1, NLT)

7. T or F _____ Therefore no one will be declared righteous in God's sight. (20)

   Do not enter into judgment with Your servant, for in Your sight no one living is righteous. (Psalm 143:2, NKJV)

8. _____ is given through faith in Jesus Christ. (22)

   Yet we know that a person is not justified by works of the law but through faith in Jesus Christ, so we also have believed in Christ Jesus, in order to be justified by faith in Christ and not by works of the law, because by works of the law no one will be justified. (Galatians 2:16, ESV)

9. [T or F _____ There is only one God. (30)

   Hear, O Israel: The Lord our God is one Lord. (Deuteronomy 6: 4, KJV)

   Now a mediator is not a mediator of one, but God is one. (Galatians 3:20, KJV)

Mind Meditation Checklist

10 Minutes

   A friend loves at all times, and is born, as is a brother, for adversity. (Proverbs 17:17, AMP)

L.E.A.P. 27

- Find a quiet comfortable place. Sit in a chair or on the floor with your head, neck, and back straight, but not stiff.
- Put aside all thoughts of the past and the future, and stay in the present. Focus on the verse above.
- Become aware of your breathing. With every breath you take allow your body to be filled with the Holy Spirit.
- Scan your body, starting with your feet, and work your way up, always ending with you head.
- Focus on the sensation of air moving in and out of your body as you breathe. Release all your sin as you exhale and invite all of God's Spirit as you inhale.
- Pay attention to the way each breath changes and is different.
- Watch every thought of sin, worry, fear, anxiety, or hate come into your mind, and release it with every exhale.
- When any thoughts come up in your mind, don't ignore or suppress them, but simply observe them, remaining calm and collected, giving them all to the Lord.
- If you find yourself getting carried away in your thoughts, just focus back on Jesus and simply return to your breathing, inhaling the Holy Spirit with every breath.
- Remember, do not be hard on yourself when you lose focus. You are just beginning a pure form of godly meditation.
- Now as the time comes to a close, sit for a minute or two, becoming aware of where you are, and get up gradually.

IMMANUEL

Body

L.E.A.P 27 Daily Workout Log

Date (Day/Month/Year): _____

Start Time: _____

End Time: _____

Scale Weight:	
Body Fat %:	
Fitness Goal:	Strength/Muscle Building/Fat Loss/Endurance/Other:

Body Parts Trained (Circle all that apply):

Whole Body | Chest | Back | Shoulders | Legs | Calves | Biceps | Triceps | Abs | Other: _____

CARDIO/AEROBIC/CONDITIONING EXERCISE

EXERCISE	TIME	DISTANCE/INTENSITY

WEIGHT, STRENGTH & RESISTANCE TRAINING

EXERCISE	WEIGHT	SETS	REPS	REST	NOTES

DIET & NUTRITION

MEAL	FOODS EATEN	APPROXIMATE CALORIES
BREAKFAST:		
LUNCH:		
DINNER:		

SELF EVALUATION

OVERALL WORKOUT RATING (1-10)		IMPROVEMENT NOTES:	

Day 4

ENJOY EVERY MOMENT

Daily Verse

You have made known to me the ways of life; You will make me full of joy in Your presence. (Acts 2:28, NKJV)

Therefore, since we have been justified through faith, we have peace with God through our Lord Jesus Christ, through whom we have gained access by faith into this grace in which we now stand. And we boast in the hope of the glory of God. Not only so, but we also glory in our sufferings, because we know that suffering produces perseverance; perseverance, character; and character, hope. And hope does not put us to shame, because God's love has been poured out into our hearts through the Holy Spirit, who has been given to us. You see, at just the right time, when we were still powerless, Christ died for the ungodly. Very rarely will anyone die for a righteous person, though for a good person someone might possibly dare to die. But God demonstrates his own love for us in this: While we were still sinners, Christ died for us. Since we have now been justified by his blood, how much more shall we be saved from God's wrath through him! For if, while we were God's enemies, we were reconciled to him through the death of his Son, how much more, having been reconciled, shall we be saved through his life!

Not only is this so, but we also boast in God through our Lord Jesus Christ, through whom we have now received reconciliation. (Romans 5:1–11, NIV)

You have been vindicated through faith because of Jesus Christ's sacrifice for you. Now that you have accepted him into your heart, it is time to enjoy the new moments that Christ has given you. This is a new day, and it is all about the joys of your life. Sometimes you get so busy you tend to forget that you are truly alive. You tend to worry about the past or are not sure what your future holds, and in the process, the moment just passes you by. Some of us go through life and look back and ask, "Where did the last eighty years of my life go?" The loss of what is old (your past) is the opportunity of something new (your future). It's time to live for each moment and enjoy it wholeheartedly. Here are some ways you can teach yourself to live with enjoyment each and every moment.

1. You must first realize you're always in the moment from the time you get up, till you go to sleep. You will be continually in the middle of something good in your life no matter what. It could be a beautiful day while you're cutting your lawn or a wonderful afternoon with your family, or even a movie night with a loved one. You will be the judge of what moments you'd like to appreciate and no one else.

2. Take a step back when you realize you are experiencing a moment that you would like to last forever. Reflect on the moment and engrave it into your memory. Picture how happy you are, the details of the scene, and the others that are around you. Feel your emotions so you can always find this feeling again. When sticky situations arise, learn to take yourself away from it. Take a short walk, a quick break, or simply just

close your eyes and concentrate on your breathing. As you are beginning to move forward, always think about it as if it happened in the past and it's something you can laugh about now in the present.

3. Make your reentry from past to present all the time. When you think of past moments and how much you enjoyed it, you can now bring all these feelings to the present and relive them all over again. It's just that easy. This function is called appreciating the present while looking back at the past.

4. During your walk with Christ, always enjoy yourself looking around in the moment and realize you are in the middle of something great, so just appreciate it. Don't ever take your life for granted from this day forth. Make all your moments a valuable one so they can last forever in your heart through Christ.

> Come now, you who say, "Today or tomorrow we will go into such and such a town and spend a year there and trade and make a profit"—yet you do not know what tomorrow will bring. What is your life? For you are a mist that appears for a little time and then vanishes. Instead you ought to say, "If the Lord wills, we will live and do this or that." As it is, you boast in your arrogance. All such boasting is evil. So whoever knows the right thing to do and fails to do it, for him it is sin. (James 4:13–17, ESV)

> Do not boast about tomorrow, For you do not know what a day may bring forth. (Proverbs 27:1, NKJV)

Remember, you are not here forever. Like it says in James, you are just a mist and can fade away anytime. You don't have any control over it. One thing in life is inevitable, and that is death. If the Son of God died for our sins to give us life, then what makes you think you won't die? Are you more special than Jesus Christ himself?

IMMANUEL

> For the kind of sorrow God wants us to experience leads us away from sin and results in salvation. There's no regret for that kind of sorrow. But worldly sorrow, which lacks repentance, results in spiritual death. (2 Corinthians 7:10, NLT)

You have to understand that death is just a word that is used to put fear in your heart. We are told to believe that death is simply ceasing to exist, to be no more. But Jesus conquered death, and now all it means is you are on your way home—your real home. It is merely the end of your body but the beginning of your spirit with Jesus Christ. Your life is the ultimate riddle of creation awaiting a choice through your faith in Christ between heaven and hell. Death is merely the key to open one of the two gates that you earn through your decisions during your life. Which choice will it be, heaven or hell? So in the meantime while you are here on earth and just passing through this world till you get home, why not just enjoy the moments that God gave you?

> So I commended enjoyment, because a man has nothing better under the sun than to eat, drink, and be merry; for this will remain with him in his labor all the days of his life which God gives him under the sun. (Ecclesiastes 8:15, NKJV)

Look at the above passage again. Notice the word *labor* in the passage. *Labor* means "to work, sweat, and toil." How can a word like *labor* be in a passage that talks about enjoyment? That's simple: God is telling you to enjoy your everyday life. The reason is this: when you enjoy your life in good times, you are storing up good emotions in your heart to prepare yourself for when the trials come.

Never move an old property line that your ancestors established. (Proverbs 22: 29)

Don't forget to enjoy every moment in life.

LEAP Challenge 4

The challenge for today is to enjoy every moment. Don't make this challenge a choir. This is such a great emotion that we tend to take for granted. In your life, it is not about the breath you take every day. It is more about each moment that takes your breath away that makes you feel alive. It is time to enjoy every moment.

L.E.A.P. Insight

Imagine a brilliant color with a splendor through your eyes' perception, is yet imperceptible.

Imagine a fragrance so intense with an aroma your nose recognizes yet is unrecognizable.

Imagine a melody so beautiful that your ears distinguish yet is indistinguishable.

Imagine a taste so full of exuberance that your mouth's essence is yet a quintessence.

Imagine a feeling so full of embracement that your touch to believe is yet unbelievable.

Imagine a keen unexplainable intuition that you call a sixth sense yet is God's Holy Spirit.

Imagine this unimaginable domain and conceive the implications of your ways that keep you distant from this clairvoyant dwelling.

It is in Christ Jesus that the Seal of Righteousness can be received for all generations to cross the threshold into God's Kingdom.

It is through Christ Jesus by your faith that is at work within you in which you are capable to imagine the reality of living in this place called heaven.

Mind

Romans Chapter 4

1. Abraham _____ God, and it was credited to him as righteousness. (3)

   > And he believed in the Lord; and he counted it to him for righteousness. (Genesis 15:6, KJV)

2. _____ are those whose transgressions are forgiven, whose sins are covered. _____ is the one whose sin the Lord will never count against them. (7–8)

   > Blessed is he whose transgression is forgiven, whose sin is covered. Blessed is the man to whom the Lord does not impute iniquity, and in whose spirit there is no deceit. (Psalms 32:1–2, NKJV)

3. T or F _____ Abraham received Gods promise through the righteousness that comes by faith. (13)

   > Blessing I will bless you, and multiplying I will multiply your descendants as the stars of the heaven and as the sand which is on the seashore; and your descendants shall possess the gate of their enemies. In your seed all the nations of the earth shall be blessed, because you have obeyed My voice. (Genesis 22:17–18, NKJV)

   > And if you are Christ's, then you are Abraham's offspring, heirs according to promise. (Galatians 3:29, ESV)

4. _____ means nothing and the promise is _____. (14)

For if the inheritance comes by the law, it no longer comes by promise; but God gave it to Abraham by a promise. (Galatians 3:18, ESV)

5. T or F _____ Therefore, the promise comes by faith. (16)

Therefore know that only those who are of faith are sons of Abraham. (Galatians 3:7, NKJV)

6. T or F _____ Abraham was the father of many nations. (17)

No longer shall your name be called Abram, but your name shall be Abraham; for I have made you a father of many nations. (Genesis 17:5, NKJV)

7. _____ was delivered over to death for our sins and was raised to life for our justification. (25)

Surely He has borne our griefs and carried our sorrows; yet we esteemed Him stricken,
     Smitten by God, and afflicted. But He was wounded for our transgressions, He was bruised for our iniquities; the chastisement for our peace was upon Him, and by His stripes we are healed. (Isaiah 53:4–5, NKJV)

Mind Meditation Checklist

10 Minutes

Children, obey your parents in the Lord [as His representatives], for this is just and right. Honor (esteem and value as precious) your father and your mother—this is the first commandment with a promise—That all may be well with you and that you may live long on the earth. Fathers, do not irritate and provoke your children to anger [do not

IMMANUEL

exasperate them to resentment], but rear them [tenderly]
in the training and discipline and the counsel and admoni-
tion of the Lord. (Ephesians 6:1–4, AMP)

- Find a quiet, comfortable place. Sit in a chair or on the floor with your head, neck, and back straight, but not stiff.
- Put aside all thoughts of the past and the future, and stay in the present. Focus on the verse above.
- Become aware of your breathing. With every breath you take, allow your body to be filled with the Holy Spirit.
- Scan your body, starting with your feet, and work your way up, always ending with your head.
- Focus on the sensation of air moving in and out of your body as you breathe.
- Release all your sins as you exhale, and invite all of God's Spirit as you inhale.
- Pay attention to the way each breath changes and is different.
- Watch every thought of sin, worry, fear, anxiety, or hate come into your mind, and release it with every exhale.
- When any thoughts come up in your mind, don't ignore or suppress them, but simply observe them, remaining calm and collective, giving them all to the Lord.
- If you find yourself getting carried away in your thoughts, just focus back on Jesus and simply return to your breathing, inhaling the Holy Spirit with every breath.
- Remember, do not be hard on yourself when you lose focus. You are just beginning a pure form of godly meditation.
- Now as the time comes to a close, sit for a minute or two, becoming aware of where you are, and get up gradually.

L.E.A.P. 27

Body

L.E.A.P 27 Daily Workout Log

Date (Day/Month/Year): _____

Start Time: _____

End Time: _____

Scale Weight:	
Body Fat %:	
Fitness Goal:	Strength/Muscle Building/Fat Loss/Endurance/Other:

Body Parts Trained (Circle all that apply):

Whole Body | Chest | Back | Shoulders | Legs | Calves | Biceps | Triceps | Abs | Other: _____

CARDIO/AEROBIC/CONDITIONING EXERCISE

EXERCISE	TIME	DISTANCE/INTENSITY

WEIGHT, STRENGTH & RESISTANCE TRAINING

EXERCISE	WEIGHT	SETS	REPS	REST	NOTES

DIET & NUTRITION

MEAL	FOODS EATEN	APPROXIMATE CALORIES
BREAKFAST:		
LUNCH:		
DINNER:		

SELF EVALUATION

OVERALL WORKOUT RATING (1-10)		IMPROVEMENT NOTES:	

Day 5

ACCEPT ANY SITUATION

Daily Verse

In the hope that I may somehow arouse my own people to envy and save some of them. For if their rejection brought reconciliation to the world, what will their acceptance be but life from the dead? If the part of the dough offered as first fruits is holy, then the whole batch is holy; if the root is holy, so are the branches. (Romans 11:14–16, NIV)

Then Jesus said to his disciples: "Therefore I tell you, do not worry about your life, what you will eat; or about your body, what you will wear. For life is more than food, and the body more than clothes. Consider the ravens: They do not sow or reap, they have no storeroom or barn; yet God feeds them. And how much more valuable you are than birds! Who of you by worrying can add a single hour to your life? Since you cannot do this very little thing, why do you worry about the rest? "Consider how the wild flowers grow. They do not labor or spin. Yet I tell you, not even Solomon in all his splendor was dressed like one of these. If that is how God clothes the grass of the field, which is here today, and tomorrow is thrown into the fire, how much more will he clothe you—you of little faith!

And do not set your heart on what you will eat or drink; do not worry about it. For the pagan world runs after all such things, and your Father knows that you need them. But seek his kingdom, and these things will be given to you as well. (Luke 12:22–31, NIV)

You are learning each step in depth. You love everyone, enjoy every moment, and now our third step that you will learn about today is "Accept any situation." What? Why? "But…you don't understand" is probably what you're thinking at this point. To align your soul, mind, and body, one starts with the knowledge and wisdom of acceptance. The first thing you have already accepted is the greatest gift that God has given you: Jesus Christ! So you are already making good progress.

For the wages of sin is death, but the free gift of God is eternal life in Christ Jesus our Lord. (Romans 6: 23, ESV)

For a lot of us, accepting this gift is so hard. Imagine someone close to you whose birthday is today. The one thing you want to do is get something special for that person, a gift that will leave them breathless. You go pick out a gift from your heart and then give it to that person. When they open the gift, they are so excited about it. It was what they have always wanted. But then, in that moment, they reach into their pocket and pull out some money and hand it to you. How would that make you feel? They try to pay you for the gift that you got with all your heart and gave to them. That is how God feels when we do the same to him.

Sometimes it is hard to accept this gift when times are tough. But you need to remember, if we can accept the good, we must accept the bad. Sometimes the bad is just a learning experience meant to strengthen us for what is to come. This reminds me of an old ancient Taoist Proverb. The story starts like this…

One day, a farmer's horse ran away. His neighbors expressed sympathy, "What terrible luck that you lost your horse!" The farmer replied, "Maybe so, maybe not."

A few days later, the horse returned, leading several wild horses. The neighbors shouted, "Your horse has returned, and brought more with him. What great fortune!" The farmer replied, "Maybe so, maybe not."

Later that week, the farmer's son was trying to break one of the wild horses and got thrown to the ground, breaking his leg. The villagers cried, "Your son broke his leg, what a calamity!" The farmer replied, "Maybe so, maybe not."

A few weeks later, soldiers from the national army marched through town, conscripting all the able-bodied young men for the army. They did not take the farmer's son because of his broken leg. Friends shouted, "Your boy is spared, what tremendous luck!" To which the farmer replied, "Maybe so, maybe not."

Isn't it amazing how simple accepting any situation can be? You don't have to get excited when great things happen or even mad when bad comes your way. You just have to learn to just accept each moment and see what is in store for the next. Can you learn to do that? "Maybe so, maybe not." Let's see what the word of God has to say on the subject matter.

> But he said to her, You speak as one of the impious and foolish women would speak. What? Shall we accept [only] good at the hand of God and shall we not accept [also] misfortune and what is of a bad nature? In [spite of] all this, Job did not sin with his lips. (Job 2:10, AMP)

Have you given your life to Christ? In this day and age, we all tend to be selfish when we think that we should give our life to Christ. He doesn't want our life, but Christ gave his life to us, and he just wants us to accept that. Why is this such a hard concept to follow?

IMMANUEL

My son, if you receive my words, and treasure my commands within you, so that you incline your ear to wisdom, and apply your heart to understanding; Yes, if you cry out for discernment, and lift up your voice for understanding, if you seek her as silver, and search for her as for hidden treasures; Then you will understand the fear of the Lord, and find the knowledge of God.

For the Lord gives wisdom; from His mouth come knowledge and understanding; He stores up sound wisdom for the upright; He is a shield to those who walk uprightly; He guards the paths of justice, and preserves the way of His saints. Then you will understand righteousness and justice, equity and every good path. (Proverbs 2:1–9, NKJV)

Moreover, when God gives someone wealth and possessions, and the ability to enjoy them, to accept their lot and be happy in their toil—this is a gift of God. They seldom reflect on the days of their life, because God keeps them occupied with gladness of heart. (Ecclesiastes 5:19–20, NIV)

He is giving us such a special gift—the gift of eternal life—and we try to buy it from him. This is a gift that we can't buy; it's only a gift that we can accept with our heart. Are you ready to accept the gift of life? Before you decide to accept this gift; reminisce on the beginning of time. Reflect on the detailed fact that God created human beings in which he left them free to do as they wished. This is called your free will and it was the birth of it. Only if you want through your free will; can you accept God's gift and decide whether you will be loyal to Him or not. He has placed fire and water before you; but it is up to you to reach out and take whichever you want. You have a choice between life and death; and in your choice you will surely get whichever you decide.

Behold, I stand at the door and knock. If anyone hears my voice and opens the door, I will come in to him and eat with him, and he with me. (Revelations 3:20, ESV)

Your Savior is asking you if you are ready. Are you ready to open the door to salvation? Are you ready to accept his gift?

When you are willing to accept Christ in your life, now you come to realize you are not of this world anymore. You were made for something far greater than what this world has to offer you. World problems become a thing of the past. Are you behind on bills, needing a job, suffering through a loss, having relationship problems, or just not understanding what's going on in your life? This is a heavy load to be carried by you alone. These are all good reasons to be concerned with. But when you learn to accept Christ in your life, you learn he wants to take the load off your back and carry them for you. You have to realize that you don't have control of these situations in your life and it's time to just let go. Give up the stress that life gives you to the Lord, and sit back and watch him work in your life. You keep leaving Christ on the sidelines, your MVP all-star player of all time, while you're trying to play in the game of life. Doesn't really make any sense does it? It's time to put Christ in the game, and he always has a few tricks up his sleeve to make life easier. All you have to do is just accept him.

Show me someone who does a good job, and I will show you someone who is better than most and worthy of the company of kings. (Proverbs 23:1–3)

Don't forget to "accept any situation."

LEAP Challenge 5

Well, after you put this book down, there is something that is going to happen to you. It doesn't matter if it's good or bad, because it is already happening. God is at the end of your life, watching all your outcomes and decisions in your life. Unless you can stop time, which you can't, you will need to learn to accept any and all situations on this wonderful day. Today, study the art of acceptance and put it into practice all day. When you acquire this gift, you will truly find that acceptance is such a beautiful art form created by God and distributed through Jesus Christ.

L.E.A.P. insight

Though you are in a dark room all alone, there is always a light switch. You may stumble, trip, fall, even get bruised trying to find this switch, but when you turn it on, the whole room lights up and you begin to see all the obstacles that were in your way, so the next time the light goes off and you're back in the dark, it will become much easier to find the switch with fewer injuries.

> You, Lord, are my lamp; the Lord turns my darkness into light.
>
> —2 Samuel 22:29 NIV

Mind

Romans Chapter 5

1. But God demonstrates his own love for us in this: While we were still _____, Christ died for us. (8)

   > This is a faithful saying, and worthy of all acceptation, that Christ Jesus came into the world to save sinners; of whom I am chief. (1 Timothy 1:15, KJV)

2. Sin entered the world through which man? (12)

   _____

And when the woman saw that the tree was good for food, and that it was pleasant to the eyes, and a tree to be desired to make one wise, she took of the fruit thereof, and did eat, and gave also unto her husband with her; and he did eat. (Genesis 3:6, KJV)

3. For as by one man's disobedience many were made sinners, so by the obedience of one shall many be made _____. (19)

And when he comes, he will convict the world of its sin, and of God's righteousness, and of the coming judgment. (John 16:8, NLT)

4. What abounds much more where sin abounds? (20)

_____

For by grace you have been saved through faith. And this is not your own doing; it is the gift of God, not a result of works, so that no one may boast. (Ephesians 2:8–9, ESV)

Mind Meditation Checklist

10 Minutes

And the grace (unmerited favor and blessing) of our Lord [actually] flowed out superabundantly and beyond measure for me, accompanied by faith and love that are [to be realized] in Christ Jesus. The saying is sure and true and worthy of full and universal acceptance, that Christ Jesus (the Messiah) came into the world to save sinners, of whom I am foremost. But I obtained mercy for the reason that in me, as the foremost [of sinners], Jesus Christ might show forth and display all His perfect long–suffering and patience for an example to [encourage] those who would thereafter believe on Him for [the gaining of] eternal life. (1Timothy 1:14–16, AMP)

- Find a quiet, comfortable place. Sit in a chair or on the floor with your head, neck, and back straight, but not stiff.
- Put aside all thoughts of the past and the future, and stay in the present. Focus on the verse above.
- Become aware of your breathing. With every breath you take, allow your body to be filled with the Holy Spirit.
- Scan your body, starting with your feet, and work your way up, always ending with you head.
- Focus on the sensation of air moving in and out of your body as you breathe. Release all your sin as you exhale and invite all of God's Spirit as you inhale.
- Pay attention to the way each breath changes and is different.
- Watch every thought of sin, worry, fear, anxiety, or hate come into your mind, and release it with every exhale.
- When any thoughts come up in your mind, don't ignore or suppress them, but simply observe them, remaining calm and collective giving them all to the Lord.
- If you find yourself getting carried away in your thoughts, just focus back on Jesus and simply return to your breathing, inhaling the Holy Spirit with every breath.
- Remember, do not be hard on yourself when you lose focus. You are just beginning a pure form of godly meditation.
- Now as the time comes to a close, sit for a minute or two, becoming aware of where you are, and get up gradually.

L.E.A.P. 27

Body

L.E.A.P 27 Daily Workout Log

Date (Day/Month/Year): _____

Start Time: _____

End Time: _____

Scale Weight:	
Body Fat %:	
Fitness Goal:	Strength/Muscle Building/Fat Loss/Endurance/Other:

Body Parts Trained (Circle all that apply):

Whole Body | Chest | Back | Shoulders | Legs | Calves | Biceps | Triceps | Abs | Other: _____

CARDIO/AEROBIC/CONDITIONING EXERCISE

EXERCISE	TIME	DISTANCE/INTENSITY

WEIGHT, STRENGTH & RESISTANCE TRAINING

EXERCISE	WEIGHT	SETS	REPS	REST	NOTES

DIET & NUTRITION

MEAL	FOODS EATEN	APPROXIMATE CALORIES
BREAKFAST:		
LUNCH:		
DINNER:		

SELF EVALUATION

OVERALL WORKOUT RATING (1-10)		IMPROVEMENT NOTES:	

Day 6

PRAISE GOD AND GIVE PEACE

Daily Verse

And he hath put a new song in my mouth, even praise unto our God: many shall see it, and fear, and shall trust in the Lord. (Psalm 40:3, KJV)

Keep on loving one another as brothers and sisters. Do not forget to show hospitality to strangers, for by so doing some people have shown hospitality to angels without knowing it. Continue to remember those in prison as if you were together with them in prison, and those who are mistreated as if you yourselves were suffering. Marriage should be honored by all, and the marriage bed kept pure, for God will judge the adulterer and all the sexually immoral. Keep your lives free from the love of money and be content with what you have, because God has said,

"Never will I leave you; never will I forsake you." So we say with confidence, "The Lord is my helper; I will not be afraid. What can mere mortals do to me?" Remember your leaders, who spoke the word of God to you. Consider the outcome of their way of life and imitate their faith. Jesus Christ is the same yesterday and today and forever.

Do not be carried away by all kinds of strange teachings. It is good for our hearts to be strengthened by grace, not by eating ceremonial foods, which is of no benefit to those who do so. We have an altar from which those who minister at the tabernacle have no right to eat. The high priest carries the blood of animals into the Most Holy Place as a sin offering, but the bodies are burned outside the camp. And so Jesus also suffered outside the city gate to make the people holy through his own blood. Let us, then, go to him outside the camp, bearing the disgrace he bore. For here we do not have an enduring city, but we are looking for the city that is to come. Through Jesus, therefore, let us continually offer to God a sacrifice of praise—the fruit of lips that openly profess his name. And do not forget to do good and to share with others, for with such sacrifices God is pleased. Have confidence in your leaders and submit to their authority, because they keep watch over you as those who must give an account. Do this so that their work will be a joy, not a burden, for that would be of no benefit to you. (Hebrews 13:1–17, NIV)

For the past three days, you have read and understood what it meant to love everyone, enjoy every moment, and accept any situation. And now you are on your last piece of this spiritual mantra: "Praise God and give peace." This is the time to give God all the glory and praise. He has saved you from death (sin), he has shown you a way out of your misery, and he has given you peace in your life, that the only thing you can do is just simply praise and worship him with all your heart. How can I praise God? The answer is a lot simpler than you may think. First you need to stop putting your limitations on Gods limitless power and realize that God is greater than my...

1. Fears
2. Circumstances

L.E.A.P. 27

3. Past
4. Limitations

And finally YOU.

When you come to appreciate that, you are showing a definitive display of praise and worship to God by trusting in Him in all that you do.

> He is your praise, and He is your God, who has done for you these great and awesome things which your eyes have seen. (Deuteronomy 10:21, NKJV)

> Rejoice in the Lord, O you righteous! For praise from the upright is beautiful. (Psalms 33:1, NKJV)

> I will bless the Lord at all times; his praise shall continually be in my mouth. My soul makes its boast in the Lord; let the humble hear and be glad. Oh, magnify the Lord with me, and let us exalt his name together! (Psalms 34:1–3, ESV)

> Let the heaven and earth praise him, the seas, and everything that moveth therein. (Psalms 69:34, KJV)

> Yes, you have been with me from birth; from my mother's womb you have cared for me. No wonder I am always praising you! (Psalms 71:6, NLT)

> Do not keep silent, O God of my praise! (Psalms 109:1, NKJV)

There are many more verses on praise. It is your time to give him all the glory. These four elements in your life is the absolute

IMMANUEL

truth of your own personal happiness. The absolute truth implies three things:

1. Whatever is true at one time and in one place is true at all times and in all places.
2. Whatever is true for one person is true for all people.
3. It also means that there are many wrong answers but only one true answer.

In other words, it's like a math problem; for example, with the equation of $1 + 1 = 2$. The answer of 2 is the absolute truth of the equation, but it also has many wrong answers in its place. In this sense, we have been living the wrong equation in our lives and getting a lot of wrong answers in its place. The absolute truth equation in life is this:

> Loving + Enjoying + Accepting + Praising = Absolute True Peace and Happiness
>
> Peace I leave with you, my peace I give unto you: not as the world giveth, give I unto you. Let not your heart be troubled, neither let it be afraid. (John 14:27, KJV)

The equation of life is now complete. This is how God intended life to be, very plain and simple. Let's love others while enjoying new life by accepting any situation that may come through praising God so we can have our true peace and happiness that has been hidden from us by this world. Now that you know the meaning of LEAP, it is time to share it with others of the world. It all starts with a 100 percent trust in Jesus, who died on the cross for your sins to build that perfect peace. The peace will now rule your heart from here and forevermore.

> And let the peace of God rule in your hearts, to which also you were called in one body; and be thankful. Let the

| 106 |

word of Christ dwell in you richly in all wisdom, teaching and admonishing one another in psalms and hymns and spiritual songs, singing with grace in your hearts to the Lord. And whatever you do in word or deed, do all in the name of the Lord Jesus, giving thanks to God the Father through Him. (Colossians 3:15–17, NKJV)

When you sit down to eat with someone important, keep in mind who he is. If you have a big appetite, restrain yourself. Don't be greedy for the fine food he serves; he may be trying to trick you. (Proverbs 23:4-5)

Don't forget to praise God and give peace today.

LEAP Challenge 6

Praising God is the key for today. Take the time to give thanks to God for all the things he gives you today in your meditation. Your way of thinking is starting to change, so give thanks, whether in good times or bad. Go out and share your praise through your interactions with others. It all starts with you.

L.E.A.P. Insight

Here is what all both human and animal must face in life: death, violence, conflict, murder, disaster, famine, sickness, and epidemic. All these things were created because of the wicked hearts of man; they are the ones who have caused destruction. Everything that comes from the earth goes back to the earth, just as all water flows into the sea. Without God we are hopeless, so I will choose to give him the praise and glory forever.

> Then I will return to my lair until they have borne their guilt and seek my face—in their misery they will earnestly seek me."
>
> —Hosea 5:15 NIV

Mind

Romans Chapter 6

1. T or F _____ Christ had to die for us to have a new life. (4)

   Buried with him in baptism, wherein also ye are risen with him through the faith of the operation of God, who hath raised him from the dead. (Colossians 2:12, KJV)

2. We should not allow _____ to reign in our bodies. (12)

   Blessed is the man who walks not in the counsel of the ungodly, Nor stands in the path of sinners, Nor sits in the seat of the scornful. (Psalm 1:1, NKJV)

3. _____ is the wages of sin. (23)

   The labor of the righteous leads to life, the wages of the wicked to sin. (Proverbs 10:16, NKJV)

4. _____ is a gift from God. (23)

   For God so loved the world, that he gave his only begotten Son, that whosoever believeth in him should not perish, but have everlasting life. (John 3:16, KJV)

Mind Meditation Checklist

10 Minutes

   And they sold their possessions (both their landed property and their movable goods) and distributed the price among all, according as any had need. And day after day

| 108 |

they regularly assembled in the temple with united purpose, and in their homes they broke bread [including the Lord's Supper]. They partook of their food with gladness and simplicity and generous hearts, constantly praising God and being in favor and goodwill with all the people; and the Lord kept adding [to their number] daily those who were being saved [from spiritual death]. (Acts 2:45–47, AMP)

- Find a quiet, comfortable place. Sit in a chair or on the floor with your head, neck, and back straight, but not stiff.
- Put aside all thoughts of the past and the future, and stay in the present. Focus on the verse above.
- Become aware of your breathing. With every breath you take, allow your body to be filled with the Holy Spirit.
- Scan your body, starting with your feet, and work your way up, always ending with you head.
- Focus on the sensation of air moving in and out of your body as you breathe.
- Release all your sin as you exhale, and invite all of God's Spirit as you inhale.
- Pay attention to the way each breath changes and is different.
- Watch every thought of sin, worry, fear, anxiety, or hate come into your mind, and release it with every exhale.
- When any thoughts come up in your mind, don't ignore or suppress them, but simply observe them, remaining calm and collected, giving them all to the Lord.
- If you find yourself getting carried away with your thoughts, just focus back on Jesus and simply return to your breathing, inhaling the Holy Spirit with every breath.
- Remember, do not be hard on yourself when you lose focus. You are just beginning a pure form of godly meditation.
- Now as the time comes to a close, sit for a minute or two, becoming aware of where you are, and get up gradually.

IMMANUEL

Body

L.E.A.P 27 Daily Workout Log

Date (Day/Month/Year): _____

Start Time: _____

End Time: _____

Scale Weight:	
Body Fat %:	
Fitness Goal:	Strength/Muscle Building/Fat Loss/Endurance/Other:

Body Parts Trained (Circle all that apply):

Whole Body | Chest | Back | Shoulders | Legs | Calves | Biceps | Triceps | Abs | Other: _____

CARDIO/AEROBIC/CONDITIONING EXERCISE

EXERCISE	TIME	DISTANCE/INTENSITY

WEIGHT, STRENGTH & RESISTANCE TRAINING

EXERCISE	WEIGHT	SETS	REPS	REST	NOTES

DIET & NUTRITION

MEAL	FOODS EATEN	APPROXIMATE CALORIES
BREAKFAST:		
LUNCH:		
DINNER:		

SELF EVALUATION

OVERALL WORKOUT RATING (1-10)		IMPROVEMENT NOTES:	

Day 7

FAITH WITH GOOD DEEDS

Daily Verse

Live such good lives among the pagans that, though they accuse you of doing wrong, they may see your good deeds and glorify God on the day he visits us. (1 Peter 2:12, NIV)

What good is it, my brothers, if someone says he has faith but does not have works? Can that faith save him? If a brother or sister is poorly clothed and lacking in daily food, and one of you says to them, "Go in peace, be warmed and filled," without giving them the things needed for the body, what good is that? So also faith by itself, if it does not have works, is dead. But someone will say, "You have faith and I have works." Show me your faith apart from your works, and I will show you my faith by my works. You believe that God is one; you do well. Even the demons believe—and shudder! Do you want to be shown, you foolish person, that faith apart from works is useless? Was not Abraham our father justified by works when he offered up his son Isaac on the altar? You see that faith was active along with his works, and faith was completed by his works. (James 2:14–22, ESV)

IMMANUEL

Today is the day to show that you have faith in Jesus with practical evidence of sincere devotion to him and the Word of God. You will challenge your words of faith by your actions and motives. You will do this by sticking to your 27-day program and meditating and praying on God's Word. True faith is the key for the doorway to your success. Remember God doesn't just want your trust; he want's your pure faith in Jesus that He can do all things through Him and take care of all things. He wants your unbelief to stop prohibiting you from seeing His miracles. God wants you to have the same faith as you would have in a chair. Yes I said a chair. We all have faith that the reason and sole purpose for having a chair is to give us comfort and hold us up from being on the ground. But it's not until we have that unshaken belief that makes us proceed to taking the action to sit, knowing without a doubt that this chair will hold us up. Praise God by having that type of faith with the belief and watch God do his miracle for you while you praise Him.

> Now faith is the assurance of things hoped for, the conviction of things not seen. For by it the people of old received their commendation. By faith we understand that the universe was created by the word of God, so that what is seen was not made out of things that are visible. By faith Abel offered to God a more acceptable sacrifice than Cain, through which he was commended as righteous, God commending him by accepting his gifts. And through his faith, though he died, he still speaks. By faith Enoch was taken up so that he should not see death, and he was not found, because God had taken him. Now before he was taken he was commended as having pleased God. And without faith it is impossible to please him, for whoever would draw near to God must believe that he exists and that he rewards those who seek him. By faith Noah, being warned by God concerning events as yet unseen, in reverent fear constructed an ark for the saving of his household.

By this he condemned the world and became an heir of the righteousness that comes by faith. By faith Abraham obeyed when he was called to go out to a place that he was to receive as an inheritance. And he went out, not knowing where he was going. By faith he went to live in the land of promise, as in a foreign land, living in tents with Isaac and Jacob, heirs with him of the same promise. For he was looking forward to the city that has foundations, whose designer and builder is God. By faith Sarah herself received power to conceive, even when she was past the age, since she considered him faithful who had promised. Therefore from one man, and him as good as dead, were born descendants as many as the stars of heaven and as many as the innumerable grains of sand by the seashore. These all died in faith, not having received the things promised, but having seen them and greeted them from afar, and having acknowledged that they were strangers and exiles on the earth. For people who speak thus make it clear that they are seeking a homeland. If they had been thinking of that land from which they had gone out, they would have had opportunity to return. But as it is, they desire a better country, that is, a heavenly one. Therefore God is not ashamed to be called their God, for he has prepared for them a city. By faith Abraham, when he was tested, offered up Isaac, and he who had received the promises was in the act of offering up his only son, of whom it was said, "Through Isaac shall your offspring be named." He considered that God was able even to raise him from the dead, from which, figuratively speaking, he did receive him back. By faith Isaac invoked future blessings on Jacob and Esau. By faith Jacob, when dying, blessed each of the sons of Joseph, bowing in worship over the head of his staff. By faith Joseph, at the end of his life, made mention of the exodus of the Israelites and gave directions concerning his bones. By faith Moses, when he was born, was hidden for three months by his parents, because they saw that the child was beautiful, and they were not afraid of the king's edict. By faith Moses, when he was grown up, refused to be called the son of Pharaoh's daughter, choosing rather to be mistreated with the people of God than to enjoy the fleeting pleasures of sin. He considered the reproach of Christ greater wealth than the treasures of Egypt, for he was looking to the reward. By faith he left Egypt, not being afraid of the anger of the king, for he endured as seeing him who is invisible. By faith he kept the Passover and sprinkled the blood, so that the Destroyer of the first-born might not touch them. By faith the people crossed the Red Sea as on dry land, but the Egyptians, when they attempted to do the same, were drowned. By faith the walls of Jericho fell down after they had been encircled for seven days. By faith Rahab the prostitute did not perish with those who were disobedient, because she had given a friendly welcome to the spies.

And what more shall I say? For time would fail me to tell of Gideon, Barak, Samson, Jephthah, of David and Samuel and the prophets—who through faith conquered kingdoms, enforced justice, obtained promises, stopped the mouths of lions, quenched the power of fire, escaped the edge of the sword, were made strong out of weakness, became mighty in war, put foreign armies to flight. Women received back their dead by resurrection. Some were tortured, refusing to accept release, so that they might rise again to a better life. Others suffered mocking and flogging, and even chains and imprisonment. They were stoned, they were sawn in two, they were killed with the sword. They went about in skins of sheep and goats, destitute, afflicted, mistreated—of whom the world was not worthy—wandering about in deserts and mountains, and in dens and caves of the earth. And all these, though commended through their faith, did not receive what was promised, since God had provided something better for us, that apart from us they should not be made perfect. (Hebrews 11:1–40, ESV)

These are great examples of the true meaning of faith. True faith involves God in all and every circumstances. The passage above is full of remarkable stories of men's true faith in God. Your faith must be in Christ, and you must be prepared to give God total control of your life. You have to take God's Word and rely completely on what he has promised you. Our own self is petrified of not having control of a situation. If we can't grasp control of our life, then we are led to believe that we are no longer in control. That statement is very true, but who is in control then? Is God in control or the devil? In reality, God created us for a purpose, but we lost sight of the true purpose. And that purpose is that we were made to praise and worship him, plain and simple. Today, it is time for us to live our true purpose of life. What is true faith, and how do we get it?

Faith is being sure of what you want and the confidence in what you do not see. Here is a simple question for you to help you understand the statement above: do you believe there is a million dollars? Now have you actually seen it, or even held it in your hands? Most of us know there is a million dollars out in the world, but we don't have it. But by faith, you believe it's out there, and by determination, you have a chance to get it, even if you haven't seen it with your own eyes. In the same aspect, you will need to focus on something you can't see and pursue it in order to do God's deed so you can complete the task. Let your faith produce good deeds by trusting God to take care of your situation. Are you ready to give God the control of your car that is driving through life?

My brethren, count it all joy when you fall into various trials, knowing that the testing of your faith produces patience. But let patience have its perfect work, that you may be perfect and complete, lacking nothing. If any of you lacks wisdom, let him ask of God, who gives to all liberally and without reproach, and it will be given to him. But let him ask in faith, with no doubting, for he who doubts is like a wave of the sea driven and tossed by the wind. For let not that man suppose that he will receive anything from the Lord; he is a double-minded man, unstable in all his ways. (James 1:2–8, NKJV)

Be wise enough not to wear yourself out trying to get rich. Your money can be gone in a flash, as if it had grown wings and flown away like an eagle. (Proverbs 23: 6-8)

LEAP Challenge 7

Today it is time to get serious about doing good deeds for others. Challenge yourself with your faith in God's Word through your actions, and show the people around you. Go out and share your faith with some good deeds.

What can you do today?

Well, the answer is quite simple: you can do anything today as long as you do it from the heart.

- Give a ride to a friend.
- Treat someone to lunch.
- Pay it forward at a drive-through.
- Cut someone's lawn.
- Give a homeless person some food.
- Volunteer to do someone else's task.
- Let someone cut in front of you in a line.

These are just a few ideas you can do today to show your good deeds.

L.E.A.P. Insight

Jesus Christ is often represented by the fish symbol which is the symbol for sacrifice, a nourishment of people in body, mind, and spirit. He is also symbolized as the fish due to the "ichthys" Greek acronym ICThUS: Iota, Chi, Theta, Upsilon, Sigma. Iesous Christos Theou Huious Soter—this means Jesus Christ God Son Saviour.

Mind

Romans Chapter 7

1. T or F _____ I would not have known what sin was had it not been for the law. (7)

> And Moses said to the people, "Do not fear; for God has come to test you, and that His fear may be before you, so that you may not sin." (Exodus 20:20, NKJV)

> But as for thee, stand thou here by me, and I will speak unto thee all the commandments, and the statutes, and the judgments, which thou shalt teach them, that they may do them in the land which I give them to possess it. (Deuteronomy 5:31, KJV)

2. What did sin do to us? (11)

_____

> And the Lord God said unto the woman, What is this that thou hast done? And the woman said, The serpent beguiled me, and I did eat. (Genesis 3:13, KJV)

IMMANUEL

3. T or F _____ I do not understand what I do. For what I want to do I do not do, but what I hate I do. (15)

> For the flesh lusteth against the Spirit, and the Spirit against the flesh: and these are contrary the one to the other: so that ye cannot do the things that ye would. (Galatians 5:17, KJV)

4. What law did Paul say he served with his mind? (25)

_____

> Gather the people together, men and women and little ones, and the stranger who is within your gates, that they may hear and that they may learn to fear the Lord your God and carefully observe all the words of this law. (Deuteronomy 31:12, NKJV)

5. What law did Paul say he served with his flesh? (25)

_____

> But the children of the murderers he did not execute, according to what is written in the Book of the Law of Moses, in which the Lord commanded, saying, "Fathers shall not be put to death for their children, nor shall children be put to death for their fathers; but a person shall be put to death for his own sin." (2 Kings 14:6, NKJV)

Mind Meditation Checklist

10 Minutes

> Let your light so shine before men that they may see your moral excellence and your praiseworthy, noble, and good deeds and recognize and honor and praise and glorify your Father Who is in heaven. (Matthew 5:16, AMP)

- Find a quiet, comfortable place. Sit in a chair or on the floor with your head, neck, and back straight, but not stiff.
- Put aside all thoughts of the past and the future, and stay in the present. Focus on the verse above.
- Become aware of your breathing. With every breath you take, allow your body to be filled with the Holy Spirit.
- Scan your body, starting with your feet, and work your way up, always ending with your head.
- Focus on the sensation of air moving in and out of your body as you breathe.
- Release all your sin as you exhale, and invite all of God's Spirit as you inhale.
- Pay attention to the way each breath changes and is different.
- Watch every thought of sin, worry, fear, anxiety, or hate come into your mind, and release it with every exhale.
- When any thoughts come up in your mind, don't ignore or suppress them, but simply observe them, remaining calm and collected, giving them all to the Lord.
- If you find yourself getting carried away in your thoughts, just focus back on Jesus and simply return to your breathing, inhaling the Holy Spirit with every breath.
- Remember, do not be hard on yourself when you lose focus. You are just beginning a pure form of godly meditation.
- Now as the time comes to a close, sit for a minute or two, becoming aware of where you are, and get up gradually.

IMMANUEL

Body

L.E.A.P 27 Daily Workout Log

Date (Day/Month/Year): _____

Start Time: _____

End Time: _____

Scale Weight:	
Body Fat %:	
Fitness Goal:	Strength/Muscle Building/Fat Loss/Endurance/Other:

Body Parts Trained (Circle all that apply):

Whole Body | Chest | Back | Shoulders | Legs | Calves | Biceps | Triceps | Abs | Other: _____

CARDIO/AEROBIC/CONDITIONING EXERCISE

EXERCISE	TIME	DISTANCE/INTENSITY

WEIGHT, STRENGTH & RESISTANCE TRAINING

EXERCISE	WEIGHT	SETS	REPS	REST	NOTES

DIET & NUTRITION

MEAL	FOODS EATEN	APPROXIMATE CALORIES
BREAKFAST:		
LUNCH:		
DINNER:		

SELF EVALUATION

OVERALL WORKOUT RATING (1-10)		IMPROVEMENT NOTES:	

| 120 |

Day 8

ARMOR OF GOD

Daily Verse

For You have armed me with strength for the battle; You have subdued under me those who rose up against me. (Psalm 18:39, NKJV)

Finally, be strong in the Lord and in his mighty power. Put on the full armor of God, so that you can take your stand against the devil's schemes. For our struggle is not against flesh and blood, but against the rulers, against the authorities, against the powers of this dark world and against the spiritual forces of evil in the heavenly realms. Therefore put on the full armor of God, so that when the day of evil comes, you may be able to stand your ground, and after you have done everything, to stand. Stand firm then, with the belt of truth buckled around your waist, with the breast-plate of righteousness in place, and with your feet fitted with the readiness that comes from the gospel of peace. In addition to all this, take up the shield of faith, with which you can extinguish all the flaming arrows of the evil one. Take the helmet of salvation and the sword of the Spirit, which is the word of God. And pray in the Spirit

| 121 |

on all occasions with all kinds of prayers and requests. With this in mind, be alert and always keep on praying for all the Lord's people. Pray also for me, that whenever I speak, words may be given me so that I will fearlessly make known the mystery of the gospel, for which I am an ambassador in chains. Pray that I may declare it fearlessly, as I should. (Ephesians 6: 10–20, NIV)

It is now time to prepare for the battle for your soul, mind, and body. Every morning, you will need to put on the full armor of God and prepare for all circumstances that come your way. This is very important to do because you are in a spiritual warfare, and you need to be prepared. You start with the following:

Belt of Truth—This is in your everyday living of your spiritual life. God, when he speaks, speaks to you in truth, so you must do the same. When you speak to anyone who comes into your life, you need to say all things in full truth. It is by lies that weaken your faith. It is by lies that weaken your relationships. It is by lies that mask your true potential. But by the truth, you will be set free. Familiarize yourself with these lists of words. Deceit, deception, dishonesty, disinformation, distortion, evasion, fabrication, falsehood, fiction, forgery, inaccuracy, misrepresentation, myth, perjury, slander, tale, aspersion, backbiting, calumniation, calumny, defamation, detraction, fable, falseness, falsification, falsity, fib, fraudulence, guile, hyperbole, invention, libel, mendacity, misstatement, obloquy, prevarication, revilement, reviling, subterfuge, vilification, whopper, tall story, white lie, and flat out just lie can all be conquered by one word. Truth.

> Pilate saith unto him, What is truth? And when he had said this, he went out again unto the Jews, and saith unto them, I find in him no fault at all. (John 18:38, KJV)

Notice how the governor asked this question. We ask this question day in and day out. Jesus Christ is the answer. How can you tell the truth? But the only way to know truth is to know your Lord Jesus Christ.

> Jesus saith unto him, I am the way, the truth, and the life: no man cometh unto the Father, but by me. (John 14:6, KJV)

So now that you have Jesus in your heart, you are able to understand what the Voice of Truth is telling you. And now your chains are broken in Jesus Christ's name.

> Then Jesus said to those Jews who believed Him, "If you abide in My word, you are My disciples indeed. And you shall know the truth, and the truth shall make you free." (John 8:31–32, NKJV)

> And take not the word of truth utterly out of my mouth; for I have hoped in thy judgments. (Psalm 119:43, KJV)

> These are the things you shall do: Speak each man the truth to his neighbor; Give judgment in your gates for truth, justice, and peace. (Zechariah 8:16, NKJV)

> Our actions will show that we belong to the truth, so we will be confident when we stand before God. Even if we feel guilty, God is greater than our feelings, and he knows everything. (1 John 3:19–20, NLT)

> This is He who came by water and blood—Jesus Christ; not only by water, but by water and blood. And it is the Spirit who bears witness, because the Spirit is truth. (1 John 5:6, NKJV)

> I was so happy when some Christian brothers arrived and told me how faithful you are to the truth–just as you

always live in the truth. Nothing makes me happier than to hear that my children live in the truth. (3 John 1:3, NIV)

Body Armor of God's Righteousness—The question that is on your mind is this: how do we get God's righteousness? That is simple, by following these four steps:

1. Surrendering your life to his Son, Jesus Christ, and proclaiming him as your Lord and Savior.
2. Understanding that God has a plan for your life and it's up to you to follow God's plan and not yours.
3. Listening to God's voice, which is located in his Word (Bible), in music, or even in people. So listen to God's plan as you plan every day.
4. Trust in him completely with all of your soul, mind, and body.

For the Lord knoweth the way of the righteous: but the way of the ungodly shall perish. (Psalms 1:6, KJV)

I will praise the Lord according to his righteousness: and will sing praise to the name of the Lord most high. (Psalms 7:17, KJV)

The righteous is delivered out of trouble, and the wicked cometh in his stead. (Proverbs 11:8, KJV)

He who trusts in his riches will fall, But the righteous will flourish like foliage. (Proverbs 11:28, NKJV)

One who is righteous is a guide to his neighbor, but the way of the wicked leads them astray. (Proverbs 12:26, ESV)

Righteousness shall be the belt of his waist, and faithfulness the belt of his loins. (Isaiah 11:5, ESV)

| 124 |

In the way of righteousness is life: and in the pathway thereof there is no death. (Proverbs 12:28, KJV)

Let no one deceive you, my children! Whoever does what is right is righteous, just as Christ is righteous. (1 John 3:7, NIV)

Shoes of Peace—Love + enjoyment + acceptance + praise = absolute peace. Every day, you don't just dress with peace but also share it with the world. You do it daily by repeating and showing through actions the spiritual mantra that you live by: "Love everybody, enjoy every moment, accept any situation, and praise God." Pass it on.

How beautiful on the mountains are the feet of those who bring good news, who proclaim peace, who bring good tidings, who proclaim salvation, who say to Zion, "Your God reigns!" (Isaiah 52:7, NIV)

May the Lord look on you with favor and give you peace. (Numbers 6:26, NIV)

I am listening to what the Lord God is saying; he promises peace to us, his own people, if we do not go back to our foolish ways. (Psalms 85:8, NIV)

I have lived too long with people who hate peace! When I speak of peace, they are for war. (Psalms 120:6–7, NIV)

He sets the time for love and the time for hate, the time for war and the time for peace. (Ecclesiastes 3:8, NIV)

Shield of Faith—Your faith is based on the belief in what you have total confidence in and yet cannot see. You believe that Christ died on the cross for your sins; just that faith alone will bring you

IMMANUEL

more peace in your life than you can imagine. When it comes to faith always remember the chair. We don't know how it's made but in the end it holds us up from falling and gives us comfort.

> To the faithful you show yourself faithful, to the blameless you show yourself blameless. (Psalm 18:25, NIV)

> Jesus answered them, "Have faith in God. I assure you that whoever tells this hill to get up and throw itself in the sea and does not doubt in his heart, but believes that what he says will happen, it will be done for him. For this reason I tell you: When you pray and ask for something, believe that you have received it, and you will be given whatever you ask for. (Mark 11:22–24, NIV)

> What it says is this: "God's message is near you, on your lips and in your heart"–that is, the message of faith that we preach. If you confess that Jesus is Lord and believe that God raised him from death, you will be saved. For it is by our faith that we are put right with God; it is by our confession that we are saved. (Romans 10:8–10, NIV)

> To have faith is to be sure of the things we hope for, to be certain of the things we cannot see. (Hebrews 11:1, NIV)

Helmet of Salvation—You have salvation the day that you asked Jesus Christ to forgive you of your sins. Every day, you must confess the sins that you have committed. You're not perfect, and God doesn't expect you to be, but by his grace, you are saved through his Son. You are a walking example of deliverance from sin and its consequences brought to you by faith in Jesus Christ.

> Salvation is found in no one else, for there is no other name under heaven given to mankind by which we must be saved. (Acts 4:12, NIV)

He put on righteousness as his breastplate, and the helmet of salvation on his head; he put on the garments of vengeance and wrapped himself in zeal as in a cloak. (Isaiah 59:17, NIV)

Sword of Spirit—The Spirit of God flows in you by the Holy Spirit that was given to you when you were saved. You must feed your spirit daily with the Word of God. Your spirit will be fed day in and day out. This is a reminder of a story about the two wolves. One evening an old Cherokee told his grandson about a battle that goes on inside people. He said, "My son, the battle is between two "wolves" inside us all.

One is Evil. It is anger, envy, jealousy, sorrow, regret, greed, arrogance, self-pity, guilt, resentment, inferiority, lies, false pride, superiority, and ego.

The other is Good. It is joy, peace, love, hope, serenity, humility, kindness, benevolence, empathy, generosity, truth, compassion and faith."

The grandson thought about it for a minute and then asked his grandfather: "Which wolf wins?"

The old Cherokee simply replied, "The one you feed." Which one will you feed? When you are being attacked, you must pick up that Sword (Bible) and feed your Holy Spirit. Then when your Spirit is fed, it is time for you to pray and worship God in the Holy Spirit.

After they prayed, the place where they were meeting was shaken. And they were all filled with the Holy Spirit and spoke the word of God boldly. (Acts 4:31, NIV)

Don't eat at the table of a stingy person or be greedy for the fine food he serves. "Come on and have some more," he says, but he doesn't mean it. What he thinks is what he really is. You will vomit up what you have eaten, and all your flattery will be wasted. (Proverbs 23: 9)

LEAP Challenge 8

Today, keep God's armor close to you. Always keep it strong by reading God's Word. Put each piece of the armor on every day. Write what you did to put on each piece of God's armor on:

- Belt of Truth
- Body Armor of God's Righteousness
- Shoes of Peace
- Shield of Faith
- Helmet of Salvation
- Sword of Spirit

Are you prepared for battle today and every day from this point on?

L.E.A.P. Insight

To believe in a cure, there must be a disease.

To believe in life, there must be the experience of death.

To believe in love, there must be generated hate.

To believe in light, there must be a self-destructive way that hides in the dark.

To believe in heaven, there must be a fear of eternity which dwells in hell.

To believe in angels, there must be an influence by the deception of demons.

To believe in GOD, there must be suffering from the trickery hands of Satan.

To believe in life's puzzle, there must be a picture in all the pieces.

Mind

Romans Chapter 8

1. T or F _____ Christ will give life to your mortal bodies because of his Spirit who lives in you.(11)

   Don't you know that you yourselves are God's temple and that God's Spirit dwells in your midst? (1 Corinthians 3:16)

2. What is the purpose of the Holy Spirit? (15–17)

   _____

   To redeem those under the law, that we might receive adoption to sonship. Because you are his sons, God sent the Spirit of his Son into our hearts, the Spirit who calls out, "Abba, Father." So you are no longer a slave, but God's child; and since you are his child, God has made you also an heir. (Galatians 4:5–7)

   "Abba, Father," he said, "everything is possible for you. Take this cup from me. Yet not what I will, but what you will." (Mark 14:36)

3. T or F _____ For the creation was subjected to frustration. (20)

   To Adam he said, "Because you listened to your wife and ate fruit from the tree about which I commanded you, 'You must not eat from it,' "Cursed is the ground because of you; through painful toil you will eat food from it all the days of your life. It will produce thorns and thistles for you, and you will eat the plants of the field. By the sweat of your brow you will eat your food until you return to the ground, since from it you were taken; for dust you are. (Genesis 3:17–19)

4. What are we waiting for so eagerly? (23)

_____

Meanwhile we groan, longing to be clothed instead with our heavenly dwelling, because when we are clothed, we will not be found naked. For while we are in this tent, we groan and are burdened, because we do not wish to be unclothed but to be clothed instead with our heavenly dwelling, so that what is mortal may be swallowed up by life. (2 Corinthians 5:2–4)

5. T or F_____ For your sake we face death all day long; we are considered as sheep to be slaughtered. (36)

Yet for your sake we face death all day long; we are considered as sheep to be slaughtered. (Psalms 44:22)

Mind Meditation Checklist

15 Minutes

Therefore put on the full armor of God, so that when the day of evil comes, you may be able to stand your ground, and after you have done everything, to stand. (Ephesians 6: 13, NIV)

- Find a quiet, comfortable place. Sit in a chair or on the floor with your head, neck, and back straight, but not stiff.
- Put aside all thoughts of the past and the future, and stay in the present. Focus on the verse above.

| 130 |

L.E.A.P. 27

- Become aware of your breathing. With every breath you take, allow your body to be filled with the Holy Spirit.
- Scan your body, starting with your feet, and work your way up, always ending with your head.
- Focus on the sensation of air moving in and out of your body as you breathe. Release all your sin as you exhale, and invite all of God's Spirit as you inhale.
- Pay attention to the way each breath changes and is different.
- Watch every thought of sin, worry, fear, anxiety, or hate come into your mind, and release it with every exhale.
- When any thoughts come up in your mind, don't ignore or suppress them but simply observe them, remaining calm and collected, giving them all to the Lord.
- If you find yourself getting carried away in your thoughts, just focus back on Jesus and simply return to your breathing, inhaling the Holy Spirit with every breath.
- Remember, do not be hard on yourself when you lose focus. You are just beginning a pure form of godly meditation.
- Now as the time comes to a close, sit for a minute or two, becoming aware of where you are, and get up gradually.

IMMANUEL

Body

L.E.A.P 27 Daily Workout Log

Date (Day/Month/Year): _____

Start Time: _____

End Time: _____

Scale Weight:	
Body Fat %:	
Fitness Goal:	**Strength/Muscle Building/Fat Loss/Endurance/Other:**

Body Parts Trained (Circle all that apply):

Whole Body | Chest | Back | Shoulders | Legs | Calves | Biceps | Triceps | Abs | Other: _____

CARDIO/AEROBIC/CONDITIONING EXERCISE

EXERCISE	*TIME*	*DISTANCE/INTENSITY*

WEIGHT, STRENGTH & RESISTANCE TRAINING

EXERCISE	*WEIGHT*	*SETS*	*REPS*	*REST*	*NOTES*

DIET & NUTRITION

MEAL	*FOODS EATEN*	*APPROXIMATE CALORIES*
BREAKFAST:		
LUNCH:		
DINNER:		

SELF EVALUATION

OVERALL WORKOUT RATING (1-10)		**IMPROVEMENT NOTES:**	

| 132 |

Day 9

HOLY SPIRIT

Daily Verse

I baptize you with water for repentance. But after me
comes one who is more powerful than I, whose sandals I
am not worthy to carry. He will baptize you with the Holy
Spirit and fire. (Matthew 3:11, NIV)

"If you love me, keep my commands. And I will ask the
Father, and he will give you another advocate to help you
and be with you forever—the Spirit of truth. The world
cannot accept him, because it neither sees him nor knows
him. But you know him, for he lives with you and will be
in you. I will not leave you as orphans; I will come to you.
Before long, the world will not see me anymore, but you
will see me. Because I live, you also will live. On that day
you will realize that I am in my Father, and you are in me,
and I am in you. Whoever has my commands and keeps
them is the one who loves me. The one who loves me will
be loved by my Father, and I too will love them and show
myself to them." Then Judas (not Judas Iscariot) said, "But,
Lord, why do you intend to show yourself to us and not to
the world?" Jesus replied, "Anyone who loves me will obey

my teaching. My Father will love them, and we will come to them and make our home with them. Anyone who does not love me will not obey my teaching. These words you hear are not my own; they belong to the Father who sent me. "All this I have spoken while still with you. But the Advocate, the Holy Spirit, whom the Father will send in my name, will teach you all things and will remind you of everything I have said to you. Peace I leave with you; my peace I give you. I do not give to you as the world gives. Do not let your hearts be troubled and do not be afraid. "You heard me say, 'I am going away and I am coming back to you.' If you loved me, you would be glad that I am going to the Father, for the Father is greater than I. I have told you now before it happens, so that when it does happen you will believe. I will not say much more to you, for the prince of this world is coming. He has no hold over me, but he comes so that the world may learn that I love the Father and do exactly what my Father has commanded me. "Come now; let us leave." (John 14:15–31, NIV)

When Jesus died on the cross for your sins, you received a special gift from God. When you accepted him in your heart, you now have an advocate that will help you forever. That advocate is the Holy Spirit. You were not meant to do this on your own, but with the Holy Spirit inside of you, the power of grace lies within you. Always remember there is a three-part system that completes the process of the Holy Trinity.

1. *God* loved you so much that he sent his son, Jesus Christ, to die for your sins. Your sins are far too great for you to buy back your way into the Father's arm. So it is by his grace and love that allows you a way out of your sins.
2. *Jesus Christ* came down from the Father to be the sacrifice to bring you closer to the Father. He was a blameless and sinless man that by water he received the Holy Spirit, and

by the shedding of his blood, you received forgiveness from the Father. It is by the Son's obedience that gave us the opportunity to be forgiven.

3. The *Holy Spirit* is now the gift that was sent to you when you accept the death of Jesus for your sins, and you now realize you are truly forgiven. The Holy Spirit is sent to you to bring you closer to God in prayer and to protect you from your old self. And finally it is by acceptance that you can receive God's Holy Spirit.

4. The bottom line is this: God is now in charge of your life, Jesus died for you to be forgiven, and the Holy Spirit is the advocate sent from Jesus that rains inside your life. You must allow God's grace to overcome you, Jesus's obedience to shine through you, and the Holy Spirit to be accepted by you.

How do you know when the Holy Spirit is working in your life? When you hear that little voice inside you telling you something is wrong, we all like to call this a conscience. But as a Christian in this world this is known by another name, a blessed name: God's Holy Spirit. With the Spirit in your life, this is now God's promise to protect you and his seal is now set upon you. Yes, now you are stamped with God's approval. How wonderful is that?

> And you also were included in Christ when you heard the message of truth, the gospel of your salvation. When you believed, you were marked in him with a seal, the promised Holy Spirit, who is a deposit guaranteeing our inheritance until the redemption of those who are God's possession— to the praise of his glory. (Ephesians 1:13–14, NIV)

Imagine that new car in the window that you always wanted and that you bought that car through a finance company. Now that you have that car, is it really truly yours? No, it isn't yours because the title to the car is in the lienholder's hand. With that being said, they would never let you leave the dealership unless you have insurance on the car so that they can protect their merchandise.

In that same sense, you were bought and received salvation from God through Christ, and now God has the title to your existence. It is in his hands, and he is going to protect you as his own child, because that is what you are. The Holy Spirit is the insurance to the title of your soul. How wonderful is that? You get a free gift, and—even better—you are insured and protected by the biggest insurance company ever known: God. Say the chant; "Like a good neighbor God is there." Now I know that is not how it goes but it feels good knowing that the creator of the Heavens and earth is now taking the time to protect you in all shapes and forms.

> We are sure that we live in union with God and that he lives in union with us, because he has given us his Spirit. (1 John 4:13, NIV)

> Do you best to preserve the unity which the Spirit gives by means of the peace that binds you together. There is one body and one Spirit, just as there is one hope to which God has called you. (Ephesians 4:3–4, NIV)

> If you have ears, then, listen to what the Spirit says to the churches! "To those who win the victory I will give the right to eat the fruit of the tree of life that grows in the Garden of God. (Revelation 2:7, NIV)

Don't try to talk sense to a fool; he can't appreciate it. (Proverbs 23: 10–11)

LEAP Challenge 9

Today is a free-day challenge. You won't have many of these challenges, so take advantage of them. Create a challenge for yourself, and follow through with it. This is the part of the challenge that you will take all you have learned up to today and create a positive outlook on life for someone else. Let the Holy Spirit lead you today. Take a look at the L.E.A.P. insight and learn the purpose of the Holy Spirit and allow it to help create your challenge.

L.E.A.P. Insight

The 7 Divine Purposes of The Holy Spirit

1. He convicts you of sin, righteousness, and of judgment. (John 16:8-11)
2. He transforms you into an essence of splendor in the sight of God. (1 Corinthians 6:11)
3. He helps you to remember the word of God. (John 14:26)
4. He helps you to lead a godly life. (Galatians 5:22-23)
5. He gives you spiritual gifts. (1 Corinthians 12:4-7)
6. He is your guarantee, seal of approval, your insurance plan of eternal life with God. (2 Corinthians 1:21-22)
7. He empowers you to be witnesses for your Lord Jesus Christ. John (15:26)

Mind

Romans Chapter 9

1. How much sorrow did the Jew's rejection of the Gospel bring to Paul? (1–3)

_____

_____

IMMANUEL

2. Who determined which of Abraham's descendants would become the heirs of the promise given to him? (9)

_____

> But God said to him, "Do not be so distressed about the boy and your slave woman. Listen to whatever Sarah tells you, because it is through Isaac that your offspring will be reckoned. (Genesis 21:12 NIV)

3. T or F_____ At the appointed time I will return, and Sarah will have a son.

> Then one of them said, "I will surely return to you about this time next year, and Sarah your wife will have a son." (Genesis 18:10)

4. The _____ will serve the _____. (12)

> The Lord said to her, "Two nations are in your womb, and two peoples from within you will be separated; one people will be stronger than the other, and the older will serve the younger." (Genesis 25:23)

5. T or F _____ For he says to Moses, "I will have mercy on whom I have mercy, and I will have compassion on whom I have compassion. (15)

> And the Lord said, "I will cause all my goodness to pass in front of you, and I will proclaim my name, the Lord, in your presence. I will have mercy on whom I will have mercy, and I will have compassion on whom I will have compassion. (Exodus 33:19)

L.E.A.P. 27

6. "I will call them '_____' who are not my people; and I will call her '_____' who is not my loved one," (17)

> I will plant her for myself in the land; I will show my love to the one I called 'Not my loved one. I will say to those called 'Not my people' 'You are my people'; and they will say, 'You are my God.'" (Hosea 2:23)

7. T or F _____ "Unless the Lord Almighty had left us descendants, we would have become like Sodom, we would have been like Gomorrah." (29)

> Unless the Lord Almighty had left us some survivors, we would have become like Sodom, we would have been like Gomorrah. (Isaiah 1:9)

8. T or F _____ "See, I lay in Zion a stone that causes people to stumble and a rock that makes them fall, and the one who believes in him will never be put to shame." (33)

> So this is what the Sovereign Lord says: "See, I lay a stone in Zion, a tested stone, a precious cornerstone for a sure foundation; the one who relies on it will never be stricken with panic. (Isaiah 28:16)

Mind Meditation Checklist

15 Minutes

> For this is what the high and exalted One says—he who lives forever, whose name is holy: "I live in a high and holy place, but also with the one who is contrite and lowly in spirit, to revive the spirit of the lowly and to revive the heart of the contrite. (Isaiah 57:15)

IMMANUEL

- Find a quiet, comfortable place. Sit in a chair or on the floor with your head, neck, and back straight, but not stiff.
- Put aside all thoughts of the past and the future, and stay in the present. Focus on the verse above.
- Become aware of your breathing. With every breath you take, allow your body to be filled with the Holy Spirit.
- Scan your body, starting with your, feet and work your way up, always ending with your head.
- Focus on the sensation of air moving in and out of your body as you breathe.
- Release all your sin as you exhale, and invite all of God's Spirit as you inhale.
- Pay attention to the way each breath changes and is different.
- Watch every thought of sin, worry, fear, anxiety, or hate come into your mind, and release it with every exhale.
- When any thoughts come up in your mind, don't ignore or suppress them, but simply observe them, remaining calm and collected, giving them all to the Lord.
- If you find yourself getting carried away in your thoughts, just focus back on Jesus and simply return to your breathing, inhaling the Holy Spirit with every breath.
- Remember, do not be hard on yourself when you lose focus. You are just beginning a pure form of godly meditation.
- Now as the time comes to a close, sit for a minute or two, becoming aware of where you are, and get up gradually.

L.E.A.P. 27

Body

L.E.A.P 27 Daily Workout Log

Date (Day/Month/Year): _____

Start Time: _____

End Time: _____

Scale Weight:	
Body Fat %:	
Fitness Goal:	Strength/Muscle Building/Fat Loss/Endurance/Other:

Body Parts Trained (Circle all that apply):

Whole Body | Chest | Back | Shoulders | Legs | Calves | Biceps | Triceps | Abs | Other: _____

CARDIO/AEROBIC/CONDITIONING EXERCISE

EXERCISE	TIME	DISTANCE/INTENSITY

WEIGHT, STRENGTH & RESISTANCE TRAINING

EXERCISE	WEIGHT	SETS	REPS	REST	NOTES

DIET & NUTRITION

MEAL	FOODS EATEN	APPROXIMATE CALORIES
BREAKFAST:		
LUNCH:		
DINNER:		

SELF EVALUATION

OVERALL WORKOUT RATING (1-10)		IMPROVEMENT NOTES:	

| 141 |

Day 10

LIVING BY THE SPIRIT'S POWER

Daily Verse

For the Holy Spirit will teach you at that time what you should say. (Luke 12:12, NIV)

So I say, walk by the Spirit, and you will not gratify the desires of the flesh. For the flesh desires what is contrary to the Spirit, and the Spirit what is contrary to the flesh. They are in conflict with each other, so that you are not to do whatever you want. But if you are led by the Spirit, you are not under the law. The acts of the flesh are obvious: sexual immorality, impurity and debauchery; idolatry and witchcraft; hatred, discord, jealousy, fits of rage, selfish ambition, dissensions, factions and envy; drunkenness, orgies, and the like. I warn you, as I did before, that those who live like this will not inherit the kingdom of God. But the fruit of the Spirit is love, joy, peace, forbearance, kindness, goodness, faithfulness, gentleness and self-control. Against such things there is no law. Those who belong to Christ Jesus have crucified the flesh with its passions and desires. Since we live by the Spirit, let us keep in step with the Spirit. Let us not become conceited, provoking and envying each other. (Galatians 5:16–26, NIV)

How do we walk in the Spirit? Well, as it says in the above scripture, "You will not gratify the desires of the flesh." Now let's take a look at what your flesh (your own) desires and what your Spirit (God's own) desires.

Flesh (Your Own)

- Sexual immorality
- Drinking
- Drugs
- Hate
- Jealousy
- Rage
- Impurity
- Selfish ambition
- Rebellious behaviors
- Gossip
- Envy of others

Spirit (God's Own)

- Love
- Joy
- Peace
- Kindness
- Goodness
- Gentleness
- Faithfulness
- Self-control

Now if you compare the two, there are many things that the flesh and the Spirit will be in constant battle between. If you look at the list, you ask yourself, Where does true happiness lie? Is it in the flesh or in the Spirit? When you choose the Spirit of God, he will show you the way toward the path of righteousness and true absolute happiness. He was sent down to lead us into the direction that God wants us to go. You were never meant to be alone in your walk with God. Now when you choose to walk in the flesh, you tend to notice some of the consequence you face. For example, if you have sexual immorality, you risk the chance of disease or an untimely birth. If you drink or do drugs, you run the risk of getting into trouble or even worse, death. If you have rage, you could hurt someone and possibly end up in jail. Your flesh is selfish from moral standards and tells you to live without any possibilities of consequences. As for your spirit in God, it is selfless and raises you to a different moral standard and teaches you to live with understanding of purposes. Do you see the difference?

> But when he, the Spirit of truth, comes, he will guide you into all the truth. He will not speak on his own; he will speak only what he hears, and he will tell you what is yet to come. He will glorify me because it is from me that he will receive what he will make known to you. All that belongs to the Father is mine. That is why I said the Spirit will receive from me what he will make known to you." (John 16:13–15, NIV)

The Spirit will speak to you; he will guide you into knowing what God needs you to know no matter what direction life takes you. The Spirit will also strengthen you and make you whole in your time of weakness. With the fear of the Lord in your heart and the encouragement of the Holy Spirit, your blessing will increase according to your faith. The greater the faith, the greater the blessing in Jesus Christ mighty name.

> But the time is coming and is already here, when by the power of God's Spirit people will worship the Father only

IMMANUEL

by the power of his Spirit can people worship him as he really is, offering him the true worship that he wants. God is Spirit, and only by the power of his spirit can people worship him as he really is. (John 4:23–24, NIV)

Never move an old property line or take over land owned by orphans. The Lord is their powerful defender, and he will argue their case against you. (Proverbs 23: 12)

LEAP Challenge 10

You have been blessed with the Holy Spirit in your life. Listen to the Spirit's calling for you. Today, follow what the Spirit calls you to do. In order to do this, you must close your mouth, open your eyes and ears, and truly hear what God is calling you to do on this glorious day. Today, you will learn how to cooperate with the Holy Spirit. In other words, this means allowing total dependence on him and his divine resources (the Bible). Today, try to keep in step with the Spirit. All keeping in step with the Holy Spirit means is to *submit* to and *rely* on the Spirit.

May God's Spirit guide you today in Jesus Christ's mighty name.

L.E.A.P. Insight

"wind blows wherever it pleases. You hear its sound, but you cannot tell where it comes from or where it is going." (John 3:8 NIV).

Now the New Testament was written in Greek, and the Greek word for wind, pneumos, which is the same word for "spirit." Now reread the verse above and substitute the word "spirit" for the word "wind.

| 146 |

Mind

Romans Chapter 10

1. What is necessary if one is going to obtain righteousness through the law? (4–5)

> Keep my decrees and laws, for the person who obeys them will live by them. I am the Lord. (Leviticus 18:5)

> For all who rely on the works of the law are under a curse, as it is written: "Cursed is everyone who does not continue to do everything written in the Book of the Law." (Galatians 3:10)

2. T or F _____ Always say in your heart, 'Who will ascend into heaven? (6)

> It is not up in heaven, so that you have to ask, "Who will ascend into heaven to get it and proclaim it to us so we may obey it?" Nor is it beyond the sea, so that you have to ask, "Who will cross the sea to get it and proclaim it to us so we may obey it?" No, the word is very near you; it is in your mouth and in your heart so you may obey it. (Deuteronomy 30:12–14)

3. _____ who believes in him will never be put to shame. (11)

> So this is what the Sovereign Lord says: "See, I lay a stone in Zion, a tested stone a precious cornerstone for a sure foundation; the one who relies on it will never be stricken with panic." (Isaiah 28:16)

4. _____ who calls on the name of the Lord will be saved. (13)

> And everyone who calls on the name of the Lord will be saved; for on Mount Zion and in Jerusalem there will be deliverance, as the Lord has said, even among the survivors whom the Lord calls. (Joel 2:32)

Mind Meditation Checklist

15 Minutes

> Since we live by the Spirit, let us keep in step with the Spirit. Let us not become conceited, provoking and envying each other. (Galatians 5:25–26, NIV)

- Find a quiet, comfortable place. Sit in a chair or on the floor with your head, neck, and back straight, but not stiff.
- Put aside all thoughts of the past and the future, and stay in the present. Focus on the verse above.
- Become aware of your breathing. With every breath you take, allow your body to be filled with the Holy Spirit.
- Scan your body, starting with your feet, and work your way up, always ending with you head.
- Focus on the sensation of air moving in and out of your body as you breathe.
- Release all your sin as you exhale, and invite all of God's Spirit as you inhale.
- Pay attention to the way each breath changes and is different.
- Watch every thought of sin, worry, fear, anxiety, or hate come into your mind, and release it with every exhale.
- When any thoughts come up in your mind, don't ignore or suppress them but simply observe them, remaining calm and collected, giving them all to the Lord.

L.E.A.P. 27

- If you find yourself getting carried away in your thoughts, just focus back on Jesus and simply return to your breathing, inhaling the Holy Spirit with every breath.
- Remember, do not be hard on yourself when you lose focus. You are just beginning a pure form of godly meditation.
- Now as the time comes to a close, sit for a minute or two, becoming aware of where you are, and get up gradually.

IMMANUEL

Body

L.E.A.P 27 Daily Workout Log

Date (Day/Month/Year): _____

Start Time: _____

End Time: _____

Scale Weight:	
Body Fat %:	
Fitness Goal:	Strength/Muscle Building/Fat Loss/Endurance/Other:

Body Parts Trained (Circle all that apply):

Whole Body | Chest | Back | Shoulders | Legs | Calves | Biceps | Triceps | Abs | Other: _____

CARDIO/AEROBIC/CONDITIONING EXERCISE

EXERCISE	TIME	DISTANCE/INTENSITY

WEIGHT, STRENGTH & RESISTANCE TRAINING

EXERCISE	WEIGHT	SETS	REPS	REST	NOTES

DIET & NUTRITION

MEAL	FOODS EATEN	APPROXIMATE CALORIES
BREAKFAST:		
LUNCH:		
DINNER:		

SELF EVALUATION

OVERALL WORKOUT RATING (1-10)		IMPROVEMENT NOTES:	

Day 11

SPIRITUAL GIFTS

Daily Verse

Therefore you do not lack any spiritual gift as you eagerly wait for our Lord Jesus Christ to be revealed. He will also keep you firm to the end, so that you will be blameless on the day of our Lord Jesus Christ. (1 Corinthians 1:7–8, NIV)

Now about the gifts of the Spirit, brothers and sisters, I do not want you to be uninformed. You know that when you were pagans, somehow or other you were influenced and led astray to mute idols. Therefore I want you to know that no one who is speaking by the Spirit of God says, "Jesus be cursed," and no one can say, "Jesus is Lord," except by the Holy Spirit. There are different kinds of gifts, but the same Spirit distributes them. There are different kinds of service, but the same Lord. There are different kinds of working, but in all of them and in everyone it is the same God at work. Now to each one the manifestation of the Spirit is given for the common good. To one there is given through the Spirit a message of wisdom, to another a message of knowledge by means of the same Spirit, to another faith by the same Spirit, to another gifts of healing by that one Spirit, to another miraculous powers, to another prophecy, to another distinguishing between spirits, to another speaking in different kinds of tongues, and to still another the interpretation of tongues. All these are the work of one and the same Spirit, and he distributes them to each one, just as he determines. Unity and Diversity in the Body Just as a body, though one, has many parts, but all its many parts form one body, so it is with Christ. For we were all baptized by one Spirit so as to form one body—whether Jews or Gentiles, slave or free—and we were all given the one Spirit to drink. Even so the body is not made up of one part but of many. Now if the foot should say, "Because I am not a hand, I do not belong to the body," it would not for that reason stop being part of the body. And if the ear should say, "Because I am not an eye, I do not belong to the body," it would not for that reason stop being part of the body. If the whole body were an eye, where would the sense of hearing be? If the whole body were an ear, where would the sense of smell be? But in fact God has placed the parts in the body, every one of them, just as he wanted them to be. If they were all one part, where would the body be? As it is, there are many parts, but one body. The eye cannot say to the hand, "I don't need you!" And the head cannot say to the feet, "I don't need you!" On the contrary, those parts of the body that seem to be weaker are indispensable, and the parts that we think are less honorable we treat with special honor. And the parts that are unpresentable are treated with special modesty, while our presentable parts need no special treatment. But God has put the body together, giving greater honor to the parts that lacked it, so that there should be no division in the body, but that its parts should have equal concern for each other. If one part suffers, every part suffers with it; if one part is honored, every part rejoices with it. Now you are the body of Christ, and each one of you is a part of it. And God has placed in the church first of all apostles, second prophets, third teachers, then miracles, then gifts of healing, of helping, of guidance, and of different kinds of tongues. Are all apostles? Are all prophets? Are all teachers? Do all work miracles? Do all have gifts of healing? Do all speak in tongues? Do all interpret? Now eagerly desire the greater gifts. (1 Corinthians 12, NIV)

Let's take a look at this wonderful gift that the Spirit of God gives you.

Spiritual Gifts

- Wisdom
- Knowledge
- Healing
- Faith
- Teaching
- Giving
- Speaking in tongues
- Understanding tongues
- Miracles
- Prophecy
- Distinguishing between spirits
- Helping others

Each of these special gifts is from the same Holy Spirit of God. Today, you will find what spiritual gift that God's Spirit has given you. Don't be afraid of the gift; you need to embrace it and use it wholeheartedly. This gift, or as I like to call a present, is an item given to you without the expectation of payment. You can share this gift, neither in the past were everything is already gone nor in the future were your not sure what's going to happen,

IMMANUEL

but always use it in the present moment as a special "present" for someone.

> So we are to use our different gifts in accordance with the grace that God has given us. If our gift is to speak God's message, we should do it according to the faith that we have; if it is to serve, we should serve; if it is to teach, we should teach; if it is to encourage others, we should do so. Whoever shares with others should do it generously; whoever has authority should work hard; whoever shows kindness to others should do it cheerfully. (Romans 12:6–8)

Pay attention to your teacher and learn all you can. (Proverbs 23: 13–14)

LEAP Challenge 11

Today you will pray and meditate so you can ask God what your gift is. Focus on the special gift that God has given you, and start sharing your ability with the world. In sharing your gift, it will bring you strength to your Holy Spirit and an abundance of joy into your life. Remember, every gift from God is a special gift. No gift is greater than the other. Here is that list again.

Spiritual Gifts

- Wisdom
- Knowledge
- Healing
- Faith
- Teaching
- Giving
- Speaking in tongues
- Understanding tongues
- Miracles

L.E.A.P. 27

- Prophecy
- Distinguishing between spirits
- Helping others

L.E.A.P. Insight

"Sometimes we may ask God for success, and He gives us physical and mental stamina. We might plead for prosperity, and we receive enlarged perspective and increased patience, or we petition for growth and are blessed with the gift of grace. He may bestow upon us conviction and confidence as we strive to achieve worthy goals."

—David A. Bednar

Mind

Romans Chapter 11

1. T or F _____ "Lord, they have killed your prophets and torn down your altars; I am the only one left, and they are trying to kill me." (3)

   He replied, "I have been very zealous for the Lord God Almighty. The Israelites have rejected your covenant, torn down your altars, and put your prophets to death with the sword. I am the only one left, and now they are trying to kill me too." (1 Kings 19:10)

2. T or F _____ God gave them a spirit of stupor eyes that could not see and ears that could not hear, to this very day. (8)

   But to this day the Lord has not given you a mind that understands or eyes that see or ears that hear. (Deuteronomy 29:4)

IMMANUEL

The Lord has brought over you a deep sleep: He has sealed your eyes (the prophets); he has covered your heads (the seers). (Isaiah 29:10)

3. May their table become a snare and a trap, a _____ block and a retribution for them. May their _____ be darkened so they cannot see, and their backs be bent forever. (9–10)

    May the table set before them become a snare; may it become retribution and a trap. May their eyes be darkened so they cannot see, and their backs be bent forever. (Psalm 69:22–23)

4. T or F _____ The deliverer will come from Zion; he will turn godlessness away from Jacob. (26)

    "The Redeemer will come to Zion, to those in Jacob who repent of their sins," declares the Lord. (Isaiah 59:20)

5. And this is my _____ with them when I take away their _____. (27)

    By this, then, will Jacob's guilt be atoned for, and this will be the full fruit of the removal of his sin: When he makes all the altar stones to be like limestone crushed to pieces, no Asherah poles or incense altars will be left standing. (Isaiah 27:9)

6. Oh, the depth of the riches of the _____ and _____ of God! How unsearchable his judgments, and his paths beyond tracing out! (33)

    "For my thoughts are not your thoughts, neither are your ways my ways," declares the Lord. (Isaiah 55:8)

| 156 |

7. Who has known the mind of the _____? Or who has been his counselor? (34)

Who can fathom the Spirit of the Lord, or instruct the Lord as his counselor? (Isaiah 40:13)

8. Who has ever given to _____, that _____ should repay them? (35)

Who has a claim against me that I must pay? Everything under heaven belongs to me. (Job 41:11)

Mind Meditation Checklist

15 Minutes

How shall we escape if we ignore so great a salvation? This salvation, which was first announced by the Lord, was confirmed to us by those who heard him. God also testified to it by signs, wonders and various miracles, and by gifts of the Holy Spirit distributed according to his will.

It is not to angels that he has subjected the world to come, about which we are speaking. (Hebrews 2:3–5, NIV)

- Find a quiet, comfortable place. Sit in a chair or on the floor with your head, neck, and back straight, but not stiff.
- Put aside all thoughts of the past and the future, and stay in the present. Focus on the verse above.
- Become aware of your breathing. With every breath you take, allow your body to be filled with the Holy Spirit.
- Scan your body, starting with your feet, and work your way up, always ending with you head.
- Focus on the sensation of air moving in and out of your body as you breathe.

IMMANUEL

- Release all your sin as you exhale, and invite all of God's Spirit as you inhale.
- Pay attention to the way each breath changes and is different.
- Watch every thought of sin, worry, fear, anxiety, or hate come into your mind, and release it with every exhale.
- When any thoughts come up in your mind, don't ignore or suppress them but simply observe them, remaining calm and collected, giving them all to the Lord.
- If you find yourself getting carried away in your thoughts, just focus back on Jesus and simply return to your breathing, inhaling the Holy Spirit with every breath.
- Remember, do not be hard on yourself when you lose focus. You are just beginning a pure form of godly meditation.
- Now as the time comes to a close, sit for a minute or two, becoming aware of where you are, and get up gradually.

L.E.A.P. 27

Body

L.E.A.P 27 Daily Workout Log

Date (Day/Month/Year): _____

Start Time: _____

End Time: _____

Scale Weight:	
Body Fat %:	
Fitness Goal:	Strength/Muscle Building/Fat Loss/Endurance/Other:

Body Parts Trained (Circle all that apply):

Whole Body | Chest | Back | Shoulders | Legs | Calves | Biceps | Triceps | Abs | Other: _____

CARDIO/AEROBIC/CONDITIONING EXERCISE

EXERCISE	TIME	DISTANCE/INTENSITY

WEIGHT, STRENGTH & RESISTANCE TRAINING

EXERCISE	WEIGHT	SETS	REPS	REST	NOTES

DIET & NUTRITION

MEAL	FOODS EATEN	APPROXIMATE CALORIES
BREAKFAST:		
LUNCH:		
DINNER:		

SELF EVALUATION

OVERALL WORKOUT RATING (1-10)		IMPROVEMENT NOTES:	

Day 12

TEACHING HOW TO PRAY

Daily Verse

The LORD detests the sacrifice of the wicked, but the prayer of the upright pleases him. (Proverbs 15:8, NIV)

"And when you pray, do not be like the hypocrites, for they love to pray standing in the synagogues and on the street corners to be seen by others. Truly I tell you, they have received their reward in full. But when you pray, go into your room, close the door and pray to your Father, who is unseen. Then your Father, who sees what is done in secret, will reward you. And when you pray, do not keep on babbling like pagans, for they think they will be heard because of their many words. Do not be like them, for your Father knows what you need before you ask him.

"This, then, is how you should pray:

"'Our Father in heaven,
hallowed be your name,
your kingdom come,
your will be done,
on earth as it is in heaven.

Give us today our daily bread.
And forgive us our debts,
as we also have forgiven our debtors.
And lead us not into temptation,
but deliver us from the evil one.'

For if you forgive other people when they sin against
you, your heavenly Father will also forgive you. But if you
do not forgive others their sins, your Father will not forgive your sins. (Matthew 6:5–15, NIV)

How do you pray effectively? Well, let's examine this prayer in
depth so you can take a closer look at what God is trying to say:

Our Father in heaven

This is the acknowledgment that God is the Father of your
life. What does a father do for his child? He teaches you and
corrects you when you are wrong. That is a true and loving father.
You are recognizing the first person in the Holy Trinity.

He will call out to me, "You are my Father, my God, the
Rock my Savior." (Psalm 89:26, NIV)

Sons, listen to what your father teaches you. Pay attention,
and you will have understanding. What I am teaching you
is good, so remember it all. (Proverbs 4:1–2, NIV)

Hallowed be your name

God is the King of kings and the Lord of lords, so here you
are, praising his name. This is an important part of the prayer. You
are giving him praise and worship, lifting his glorious name on
high, and sanctifying the identification of God the Father.

Immediately his mouth was opened and his tongue set
free, and he began to speak, praising God. (Luke 1:64, NIV)

From the east to the west praise the name of the Lord! (Psalms 113:3, NIV)

Your kingdom come, your will be done, on earth as it is in heaven

You recognize that the kingdom of God is beyond your understanding, and you are waiting for the day that the kingdom of heaven is coming. Here you are, saying with true faith that his glorious kingdom is coming. You're acknowledging that God's will is going to be your priority and living your life on earth as you would in heaven. Heaven is beyond your understanding, so what you are trying to bring to this ordinary world is something extraordinary. All you need is to add just a little "extra" in your life.

At the time of those rulers the God of heaven will establish a kingdom that will never end. It will never be conquered, but will completely destroy all those empires and then last forever. (Daniel 2:44, NIV)

"Turn away from your sins," he said, "because the Kingdom of heaven is near!" (Matthew 3:2, NIV)

As you go, proclaim this message: "The kingdom of heaven has come near." (Matthew 10:7, NIV)

Give us today our daily bread

You are asking God to bless you each day and that you may be blessed with your daily needs, not your daily wants. Some prayers that you ask for may not be what you *need* to keep your walk with God but what you *want*. Always remember, when you started the prayer, you started with "Father," and as any parent, they will give their children what they need.

Look at the birds of the air; they do not sow or reap or store away in barns, and yet your heavenly Father feeds them.

IMMANUEL

Are you not much more valuable than they? (Matthew 6:26, NIV)

Keep falsehood and lies far from me; give me neither poverty nor riches, but give me only my daily bread. (Proverbs 30:8, NIV)

And forgive us our debts

You are asking God to forgive you of your daily sins (debts) that you have committed. This is a new start for you. It's like on day 1, when you wrote your sinful nature on paper. God too has an account of your sins, but when you ask for forgiveness, he crumples up the paper and throws it away as a fresh start for your life.

Then I confessed my sins to you; I did not conceal my wrongdoings. I decided to confess them to you, and you forgave all my sins. (Psalms 32:5, NIV)

You will never succeed in life if you try to hide your sins. Confess them and give them up; then God will show mercy to you. (Proverbs 28:13, NIV)

If we confess our sins, he is faithful and just and will forgive us our sins and purify us from all unrighteousness. (1 John 1:9, NIV)

As we have also forgiven our debtors

Now that God has forgiven you of your sins, it is time for you to forgive others of their sins that they may have committed against you. This is an important part of being forgiven from the Father. Remember that we are all God's children, so we must learn to forgive those who hurt us. Next time you feel like you can't forgive someone, go look in the mirror and tell yourself why you can't. And notice it's like God telling you right back that he can't forgive you as well. Forgiveness paints an earthly picture of what God's grace accurately stands for.

> "If you forgive others the wrongs they have done to you, your Father in heaven will also forgive you. But if you do not forgive others their sins, your Father will not forgive your sins. (Matthew 6:14–15, NIV)

> And Jesus concluded, "That is how my Father in heaven will treat every one of you unless you forgive your brother from your heart." (Matthew 18:35, NIV)

And lead us not into temptation

You are asking God to protect you from all temptation of evil. Remember, God cannot tempt you, for he is holy. The only temptation that befalls on you is the flesh (old self). Satan uses your flesh to tempt you in ways that are extreme. If you forget that, go back and read the letter from Deceit. God is here to guide you through any temptations of your flesh.

> Watch and pray so that you will not fall into temptation. The spirit is willing, but the flesh is weak. (Mark 14:38, NIV)

> No temptation has overtaken you except what is common to mankind. And God is faithful; he will not let you be tempted beyond what you can bear. But when you are tempted, he will also provide a way out so that you can endure it. (1 Corinthians 10:13, NIV)

But deliver us from the evil one

You are asking God to deliver you from the bonds of the devil. This is a hard part of the prayer to say. In this day and age, we are made to believe there is no devil. Unfortunately, if you believe in God, then there is an evil one and his name is the devil. He is the tempter of all, he is difficult, deceptive, and a problematic part of life for mankind.

> All you need to say is simply "Yes" or "No"; anything beyond this comes from the evil one. (Matthew 5:37, NIV)

> The field is the world, and the good seed stands for the people of the kingdom. The weeds are the people of the evil one. (Matthew 13:38, NIV)

> My prayer is not that you take them out of the world but that you protect them from the evil one. (John 17:15, NIV)

If we ask God in our everyday prayer through the Holy Spirit, he will give us all that we need, and more. As it says at the end of Luke 11, "How much more will your Father in heaven give the Holy Spirit to those who ask him!" (Luke 11:13, NIV).

You have to ask yourself, "Is what I am praying for guiding my spiritual walk for God or for my worldly walk for my flesh?" When you pray, you also need to be persistent.

> Then Jesus told his disciples a parable to show them that they should always pray and not give up. He said: "In a certain town there was a judge who neither feared God nor cared what people thought. And there was a widow in that town who kept coming to him with the plea, 'Grant me justice against my adversary.' "For some time he refused. But finally he said to himself, 'Even though I don't fear God or care what people think, yet because this widow keeps bothering me, I will see that she gets justice, so that she won't eventually come and attack me!'" And the Lord said, "Listen to what the unjust judge says. And will not God bring about justice for his chosen ones, who cry out to him day and night? Will he keep putting them

off? I tell you, he will see that they get justice, and quickly. However, when the Son of Man comes, will he find faith on the earth?" (Luke 18:1–8, NIV)

The more that we ask God for our daily needs, the more he hears our prayers. The final piece to a complete prayer is to ask all of this in Jesus Christ's name and to always be thankful, even before your prayers are answered. Thanking God for already answering your prayer is a sign of true faith. Praying in this manner is a faith-based prayer and not a hope-based prayer. When you pray with faith, you already know your prayers will be answered rather than hoping it will be. Learning to pray in this manner will give you all you need in abundance and more.

Don't hesitate to discipline children. A good spanking won't kill them. As a matter of fact, it may save their lives. (Proverbs 23: 15–16)

LEAP Challenge 12

Today you will focus your time on prayer by faith and not prayer by hope. Give it up to the Lord, and watch him answer your prayers in abundance. Be persistent and sit back and let God take care of the rest. Don't forget to always thank him for answering your prayers no matter what. Let all your prayers include all of the following:

- Acknowledge God the Father.
- Praise God in your prayer.
- Commit in all good deeds through prayer.
- Ask God for what you need in Jesus's name.
- Forgive others for their sin against you.
- Redemption is what is given to you through Jesus Christ.
- Thanksgiving must be shouted out for all God is going to give you through his Son, Jesus Christ.

Acknowledge, praise, commit, ask, forgive, redeem, and give thanks.

L.E.A.P. Insight

For some of us, we may think that this is truly "hell on earth" due to the misery of this world. But let God reveal to you one major factor that will plunge into your heart and never let go. On earth, no matter how bad the circumstances get, there is always hope to get you through. On the other hand, in hell there lies the eternal revelation that hope is dead and has departed far from you. So when you are having a bad day, constantly clench on the grace of God who gives us an abundance of hope in this life.

Mind

Romans Chapter 12

1. T or F _____ For just as each of us has one body with many members, and these members do not all have the same function, so in Christ we, though many, form one body, and each member belongs to all the others. (4–5)

   > Just as a body, though one, has many parts, but all its many parts form one body, so it is with Christ. (1 Corinthians 12:12)

2. What are the different gifts we have? (6–8)

   _____

   _____

   > There are different kinds of gifts, but the same Spirit distributes them. There are different kinds of service, but the same Lord. There are different kinds of working, but in

L.E.A.P. 27

all of them and in everyone it is the same God at work. Now to each one the manifestation of the Spirit is given for the common good. To one there is given through the Spirit a message of wisdom, to another a message of knowledge by means of the same Spirit, to another faith by the same Spirit, to another gifts of healing by that one Spirit, to another miraculous powers, to another prophecy, to another distinguishing between spirits, to another speaking in different kinds of tongues, and to still another the interpretation of tongues. All these are the work of one and the same Spirit, and he distributes them to each one, just as he determines. (1 Corinthians 12:4–11)

3. _____ those who persecute you; _____ and do not curse. (14)

But I tell you, love your enemies and pray for those who persecute you. (Matthew 5:44)

Bless those who curse you, pray for those who mistreat you. (Luke 6:28)

4. T or F _____ Be proud, and do not be willing to associate with people of low position. (16)

Do not be wise in your own eyes; fear the Lord and shun evil. (Proverbs 3:7)

5. Why should you not take revenge? (19)

It is mine to avenge; I will repay. In due time their foot will slip; their day of disaster is near and their doom rushes upon them. (Deuteronomy 32:35)

6. T or F _____ If your enemy is hungry, starve him; if he is thirsty, give him something to nothing.

> If your enemy is hungry, give him food to eat; if he is thirsty, give him water to drink. (Proverbs 25:21)

Mind Meditation Checklist

15 Minutes

> My steps have held to your paths; my feet have not stumbled. I call on you, my God, for you will answer me; turn your ear to me and hear my prayer. Show me the wonders of your great love, you who save by your right hand those who take refuge in you from their foes. (Psalms 17:5–7, NIV)

- Find a quiet, comfortable place. Sit in a chair or on the floor with your head, neck, and back straight, but not stiff.
- Put aside all thoughts of the past and the future, and stay in the present. Focus on the verse above.
- Become aware of your breathing. With every breath you take, allow your body to be filled with the Holy Spirit.
- Scan your body, starting with your feet, and work your way up, always ending with your head.
- Focus on the sensation of air moving in and out of your body as you breathe. Release all your sin as you exhale, and invite all of God's Spirit as you inhale.
- Pay attention to the way each breath changes and is different.
- Watch every thought of sin, worry, fear, anxiety, or hate come into your mind, and release it with every exhale.
- When any thoughts come up in your mind, don't ignore or suppress them but simply observe them, remaining calm and collected, giving them all to the Lord.

L.E.A.P. 27

- If you find yourself getting carried away in your thoughts, just focus back on Jesus and simply return to your breathing, inhaling the Holy Spirit with every breath.
- Remember, do not be hard on yourself when you lose focus. You are just beginning a pure form of godly meditation.
- Now as the time comes to a close, sit for a minute or two, becoming aware of where you are, and get up gradually.

IMMANUEL

Body

L.E.A.P 27 Daily Workout Log

Date (Day/Month/Year): _____

Start Time: _____

End Time: _____

Scale Weight:	
Body Fat %:	
Fitness Goal:	Strength/Muscle Building/Fat Loss/Endurance/Other:

Body Parts Trained (Circle all that apply):

Whole Body | Chest | Back | Shoulders | Legs | Calves | Biceps | Triceps | Abs | Other: _____

CARDIO/AEROBIC/CONDITIONING EXERCISE

EXERCISE	TIME	DISTANCE/INTENSITY

WEIGHT, STRENGTH & RESISTANCE TRAINING

EXERCISE	WEIGHT	SETS	REPS	REST	NOTES

DIET & NUTRITION

MEAL	FOODS EATEN	APPROXIMATE CALORIES
BREAKFAST:		
LUNCH:		
DINNER:		

SELF EVALUATION

OVERALL WORKOUT RATING (1-10)		IMPROVEMENT NOTES:	

Day 13

WORDS OF AUTHORITY

Daily Verse

If anyone speaks, they should do so as one who speaks the very words of God. If anyone serves, they should do so with the strength God provides, so that in all things God may be praised through Jesus Christ. To him be the glory and the power forever and ever. Amen. (1 Peter 4:11, NIV)

But what does it say? "The word is near you; it is in your mouth and in your heart," that is, the message concerning faith that we proclaim: If you declare with your mouth, "Jesus is Lord," and believe in your heart that God raised him from the dead, you will be saved. For it is with your heart that you believe and are justified, and it is with your mouth that you profess your faith and are saved. As Scripture says, "Anyone who believes in him will never be put to shame." (Romans 10:8–11, NIV)

Jesus entered the temple courts, and, while he was teaching, the chief priests and the elders of the people came to him. "By what authority are you doing these things?" they asked. "And who gave you this authority?" Jesus replied,

IMMANUEL

"I will also ask you one question. If you answer me, I will tell you by what authority I am doing these things. John's baptism—where did it come from? Was it from heaven, or of human origin?" They discussed it among themselves and said, "If we say, 'From heaven,' he will ask, 'Then why didn't you believe him?' But if we say, 'Of human origin'—we are afraid of the people, for they all hold that John was a prophet." So they answered Jesus, "We don't know." Then he said, "Neither will I tell you by what authority I am doing these things. (Matthew 21:23–27, NIV)

In this chapter, you will learn how powerful your own words will be. Your own words could do so much in this world. They can hurt, scorn, show hate, destroy, manipulate, lie, break down the spirit, and keep others from God.

What my enemies say can never be trusted; they only want to destroy. Their words are flattering and smooth, but full of deadly deceit. (Psalms 5:9, NIV)

His speech is filled with curses, lies, and threats; he is quick to speak hateful, evil words. (Psalms 10:7, NIV)

Their tongues are like deadly snakes; their words are like a cobra's poison. (Psalms 140:3, NIV)

Their words are full of deadly deceit; wicked lies roll off their tongues, and dangerous threats, like snake's poison, from their lips; their speech is filled with bitter curses. (Romans 3:13–14, NIV)

Or they can be uplifting, praise, show love, support, build up when someone is down; it's so scary how your tongue, so minute a part of the body, is so powerful.

We all stumble in many ways. Anyone who is never at fault in what they say is perfect, able to keep their whole body in check. When we put bits into the mouths of horses to make them obey us, we can turn the whole animal. Or take ships as an example. Although they are so large and are driven by strong winds, they are steered by a very small rudder wherever the pilot wants to go. Likewise, the tongue is a small part of the body, but it makes great boasts. Consider what a great forest is set on fire by a small spark. The tongue also is a fire, a world of evil among the parts of the body. It corrupts the whole body, sets the whole course of one's life on fire, and is itself set on fire by hell. All kinds of animals, birds, reptiles and sea creatures are being tamed and have been tamed by mankind, but no human being can tame the tongue. It is a restless evil, full of deadly poison. With the tongue we praise our Lord and Father, and with it we curse human beings, who have been made in God's likeness. Out of the same mouth come praise and cursing. My brothers and sisters, this should not be. Can both fresh water and salt water flow from the same spring? My brothers and sisters, can a fig tree bear olives, or a grapevine bear figs? Neither can a salt spring produce fresh water. (James 3:2–12, NIV)

Now you know how powerful your tongue and your words truly are. It is time for you to use your words with the authority God intended for you. You now have the Holy Spirit in your life, and your words are more powerful than ever. In order to bring your powerful words to life it will take three steps to receive the power of authority in your words:

1. Confidence in your heart that what you are saying is from the Holy Spirit.
2. Faith in what you are saying.

3. Assurance that when you speak, you speak the words as if they have already happened.

> Early in the morning, as Jesus was on his way back to the city, he was hungry. Seeing a fig tree by the road, he went up to it but found nothing on it except leaves. Then he said to it, "May you never bear fruit again!" Immediately the tree withered. When the disciples saw this, they were amazed. "How did the fig tree wither so quickly?" they asked. Jesus replied, "Truly I tell you, if you have faith and do not doubt, not only can you do what was done to the fig tree, but also you can say to this mountain, 'Go, throw yourself into the sea,' and it will be done. If you believe, you will receive whatever you ask for in prayer." (Matthew 21:18–22, NIV)

Jesus said, "May you never bear fruit again!" Then the fig tree withered away. He didn't ask the tree. He had the confidence in his words, which led to faith in his heart and the assurance that when he commanded it, it was already done. That is how your life should be. Your words should speak with confidence, faith, and assurance. You need to start taking control of what comes out of your mouth and commanding all your heart with the belief that God will give you what you need. When you ask in Jesus's name, it will be answered, not in your time but God's time. Take a look at Genesis 1 and 2 and notice God didn't just create the world but spoke it into existence:

> And God said, "Let there be light," and there was light.
> And God said, "Let there be a vault between the waters to separate water from water."
> And God said, "Let the water under the sky be gathered to one place, and let dry ground appear." And it was so.

Then God said, "Let the land produce vegetation: seed-bearing plants and trees on the land that bear fruit with seed in it, according to their various kinds." And it was so.

And God said, "Let there be lights in the vault of the sky to separate the day from the night, and let them serve as signs to mark sacred times, and days and years, and let them be lights in the vault of the sky to give light on the earth." And it was so.

And God said, "Let the water teem with living creatures, and let birds fly above the earth across the vault of the sky."

And God said, "Let the land produce living creatures according to their kinds: the livestock, the creatures that move along the ground, and the wild animals, each according to its kind." And it was so.

Then God said, "Let us make mankind in our image, in our likeness, so that they may rule over the fish in the sea and the birds in the sky, over the livestock and all the wild animals,[a] and over all the creatures that move along the ground." So God created mankind in his own image, in the image of God he created them; male and female he created them.

—INSERTS FROM Genesis 1and2, NIV

You were made in God's image. You are a special gift created by God, so don't forget that. When God spoke, he spoke with authority, and it was made. You now have Jesus in your heart, who died on the cross for your sins and who sent you the Holy Spirit to guide you on your spiritual path. You have God's spirit over you, so when you ask God, understand that you will get your prayers answered, when you ask with confidence, faith, and assurance in Christ Jesus's name. You just have to confess it boldly and faithfully as if your prayers have already been answered.

Everything that you say in life is planting a seed either in your heart or in the heart of others. For example, when you are sick, do you plant that seed in your heart and acknowledge you are sick by confessing it with your mouth? As soon as you confess you are sick, do you not feel worse? What about when you wake up in the morning and see that it is raining outside and you tell yourself it is going to be a bad day? How does that day turn out for you? You already accept in your heart that you are sick, or you are going to have a bad day, and then you confess it with your mouth; then if anything happens, you react to it with what you planted in your heart.

Today will be the day that you will speak positive words to yourself and others with the bold confidence of Jesus Christ who sends God's spirit to rain over you.

My child, if you become wise, I will be very happy. I will be proud when I hear you speaking words of wisdom. (Proverbs 23: 17–18)

LEAP Challenge 13

Try something new today, confess with your mouth that today is going to be a blessed day, and go out and experience your day. Remember, you are still living by your mantra: love everybody, enjoy every moment, accept any situation, praise God, and give peace. Living in this manner will lower your own personal stress level. God knows how powerful words are, so start by living your life of truthful and positive words today and forevermore.

L.E.A.P Insight

Our Father, what a marvel this book and your Bible is. How wonderful that we should have it in our hands, and what a terrible tragedy that we should let it lie unopened, unread, unstudied week after week. Wake us up, Lord. Help us to realize that here, by means of the Spirit interpreting it to us, you have given adequate and full knowledge to meet every devious and subtly deceitful philosophy in our world today. Make us men and women of the book to live by with your Bible as a guideline. Bring us back to it. We pray in Jesus's name, amen.

Mind

Romans Chapter 13

1. T or F _____ Take from everyone even if you owe them: If you owe taxes, don't pay taxes; if revenue, then revenue; if respect, then respect; if honor, then honor.

   Then he said to them, "So give back to Caesar what is Caesar's, and to God what is God's." (Matthew 22:21)

2. What are all the commandments summed up in to?

   _____

   Do not seek revenge or bear a grudge against anyone among your people, but love your neighbor as yourself. I am the Lord. (Leviticus 19:18)

Mind Meditation Checklist

15 Minutes

   My mouth will speak words of wisdom; the meditation of my heart will give you understanding. (Psalm 49:3, NIV)

- Find a quiet, comfortable place. Sit in a chair or on the floor with your head, neck, and back straight, but not stiff.
- Put aside all thoughts of the past and the future, and stay in the present. Focus on the verse above.
- Become aware of your breathing. With every breath you take, allow your body to be filled with the Holy Spirit.

IMMANUEL

- Scan your body starting with your feet and work your way up always ending with you head.
- Focus on the sensation of air moving in and out of your body as you breathe. Release all your sin as you exhale and invite all of God's Spirit as you inhale.
- Pay attention to the way each breath changes and is different.
- Watch every thought of sin, worry, fear, anxiety, or hate come into your mind, and release it with every exhale.
- When any thoughts come up in your mind, don't ignore or suppress them but simply observe them, remaining calm and collected, giving them all to the Lord.
- If you find yourself getting carried away in your thoughts, just focus back on Jesus and simply return to your breathing, inhaling the Holy Spirit with every breath.
- Remember, do not be hard on yourself when you lose focus. You are just beginning a pure form of godly meditation.
- Now as the time comes to a close, sit for a minute or two, becoming aware of where you are, and get up gradually.

L.E.A.P. 27

Body

L.E.A.P 27 Daily Workout Log

Date (Day/Month/Year): _____

Start Time: _____

End Time: _____

Scale Weight:	
Body Fat %:	
Fitness Goal:	Strength/Muscle Building/Fat Loss/Endurance/Other:

Body Parts Trained (Circle all that apply):

Whole Body | Chest | Back | Shoulders | Legs | Calves | Biceps | Triceps | Abs | Other: _____

CARDIO/AEROBIC/CONDITIONING EXERCISE

EXERCISE	TIME	DISTANCE/INTENSITY

WEIGHT, STRENGTH & RESISTANCE TRAINING

EXERCISE	WEIGHT	SETS	REPS	REST	NOTES

DIET & NUTRITION

MEAL	FOODS EATEN	APPROXIMATE CALORIES
BREAKFAST:		
LUNCH:		
DINNER:		

SELF EVALUATION

OVERALL WORKOUT RATING (1-10)		IMPROVEMENT NOTES:	

Day 14

GOOD SAMARITAN

Daily Verse

In the same way, let your light shine before others, that they may see your good deeds and glorify your Father in heaven. (Matthew 5:16, NIV)

On one occasion an expert in the law stood up to test Jesus. "Teacher," he asked, "what must I do to inherit eternal life?" "What is written in the Law?" he replied. "How do you read it?" He answered, "'Love the Lord your God with all your heart and with all your soul and with all your strength and with all your mind'; and, 'Love your neighbor as yourself.'" "You have answered correctly," Jesus replied. "Do this and you will live." But he wanted to justify himself, so he asked Jesus, "And who is my neighbor?" In reply Jesus said: "A man was going down from Jerusalem to Jericho, when he was attacked by robbers. They stripped him of his clothes, beat him and went away, leaving him half dead. A priest happened to be going down the same road, and when he saw the man, he passed by on the other side. So too, a Levite, when he came to the place and saw him, passed by on the other side. But a Samaritan, as he traveled, came where the man was; and when he saw him, he took pity on him. He went to him and bandaged his wounds, pouring on oil and wine. Then he put the man on his own donkey, brought him to an inn and took care of him. The next day he took out two denarii and gave them to the innkeeper. 'Look after him,' he said, 'and when I return, I will reimburse you for any extra expense you may have.' "Which of these three do you think was a neighbor to the man who fell into the hands of robbers?" The expert in the law replied, "The one who had mercy on him." Jesus told him, "Go and do likewise." (Luke 10:25–37, NIV)

What ever happened to being a Good Samaritan? Do they still exist? What is a Samaritan? A Good Samaritan is a charitable or helpful person. But what truly happened to these people that were so humble of others. The truth of the matter is that we do still have them around, there is just not too many of them anymore in this thoughtless day and age. What we are seeing firsthand is the extinction of an optimistic race towards others. We all lack the true qualities of what God's definition of a Samaritan is. Ask yourself these questions and see if you are up to help God's people.

1. Can I think independently?
2. Can I act in a responsible manner?
3. Do I stand up for what is right no matter the consequences?
4. Am I truly afraid of what society will say?
5. Am I afraid to "ruffle a few feathers" or "go against the grain" when someone is in need?

Being a Good Samaritan is more than just giving money, it means you must put yourself last and courageously take action on putting all others first. Ouch. "You mean I have to worry about others more than my own emotions and feelings." Yes, this is the accurate meaning of what God needs you to do for others.

Jesus told them at the end of the parable, "You go, and do likewise." Today you have to learn to show mercy and compassion to those who have less than you have. We were created to praise and worship as well as take care of God's children and everyone in this world, both good and bad are God's children.

> Keep on loving one another as brothers and sisters. Do not forget to show hospitality to strangers, for by so doing some people have shown hospitality to angels without knowing it. Continue to remember those in prison as if you were together with them in prison, and those who are mistreated as if you yourselves were suffering. (Hebrews 13:1–3, NIV)

It is important not to forget to show that you are loving and caring toward others in your actions. Whether it be giving someone some money for a meal, paying for some groceries for someone, or giving a simple bottle of water to someone. You never know who you may be helping at that moment. Either way you look at it, your rewards in heaven and here on earth will be blessed. The more God gives you, the more you should give back to God's people and all are God's people, who are in need of it. We all lack this quality of life that God intended for us to have through the preparation and teaching of his Son Jesus Christ. We are here to lead and take care of all God's children.

> The Lord is righteous and loves good deeds; those who do them will live in his presence. (Psalms 11:7, NIV)

> And the four men were appointed to provide the prisoners with clothing from the captured loot. They gave them clothes and sandals to wear, gave them enough to eat and drink, and put olive oil on their wounds. Those who were too weak to walk were put on donkeys. (2 Chronicles 28:15, NIV)

IMMANUEL

Jesus said to them, "I have done many good deeds in your presence which the Father gave me to do; for which one of these do you want to stone me?" (John 10:32, NIV)

Don't be envious of sinful people; let reverence for the Lord be the concern of your life. If it is, you have a bright future. (Proverbs 23: 19-21)

LEAP Challenge 14

It's time to share that same love and compassion that the Savior gave you. Today is the day that you will become the Good Samaritan of someone's life. A Good Samaritan is someone who voluntarily does a good act or helps someone out. Will you fit that description today? It doesn't matter what you do, but don't let your busy schedule stand in the way of helping God's people.

L.E.A.P. Insight

Everything happens for a reason. Sometimes people come into our life and we know right away that they were meant to be there. They serve as some sort of purpose, to teach us a lesson or help figure out who we are or who we want to become. You never know who these people may be; your roommate, your neighbor, long lost friend, lover, or even a complete stranger who, when we link eyes with them, we know at that very moment that they will affect our life in some profound way. And sometimes, things happen to us and at the time they seem horrible, painful, and unfair, but in retrospect, we realize that without overcoming those obstacles, we would never have realized our true potential, our true strength, and our true will power of the heart. Everything happens for a reason. Nothing happens by chance or by means of good or bad luck. Illness, injury, love, lost moments, true greatness, or just sheer stupidity can all occur to test the limits of our

| 186 |

soul. Without these small tests or even big tests, life would be like a smooth paved, straight, flat road leading to nowhere. Safe and comfortable will be the travel, but dull and utterly pointless. The people we meet who affect our life's successes and downfalls, they are the ones who will define our character. Even the bad experiences can be learned from. Those lessons are the hardest to bear and yet the most important ones to teach us. If someone hurts you, betrays you, or breaks your heart…forgive them, for they have helped you learn about trust and the importance of being cautious to whom you open your heart. If someone loves you, love them back unconditionally, not only because they love you, but because they are teaching you to love and opening your heart and eyes to things you would have never seen or felt without them. Make every day count. Appreciate every moment and give nothing back. Take from it everything that you possibly can, for you may never be able to experience it again. Talk to people you have never talked to before, and actually listen, let yourself fall in love, break free, and set your sights high. You can make your life anything you wish. Create your own life and then go out and live it. I wish you all the best in your endeavors as well as struggles in life. Have a fighting spirit and never hesitate to get back in the struggle in life.

Mind

Romans Chapter 14

1. T or F _____ One person's faith allows them to eat anything, but another, whose faith is weak, eats only vegetables (2)

   > Therefore do not let anyone judge you by what you eat or drink, or with regard to a religious festival, a New Moon celebration or a Sabbath day. (Colossians 2:16)

2. For we will _____ stand before God's judgment seat. (10)

IMMANUEL

For we must all appear before the judgment seat of Christ, so that each of us may receive what is due us for the things done while in the body, whether good or bad. (2 Corinthians 5:10)

3. Every _____ will bow before me; every _____ will acknowledge God. (11)

By myself I have sworn, my mouth has uttered in all integrity a word that will not be revoked: Before me every knee will bow; by me every tongue will swear. (Isaiah 45:23)

Mind Meditation Checklist

20 Minutes

For it is by grace you have been saved, through faith—and this is not from yourselves, it is the gift of God—not by works, so that no one can boast. For we are God's handiwork, created in Christ Jesus to do good works, which God prepared in advance for us to do. (Ephesians 2:8–10, NIV)

- Find a quiet, comfortable place. Sit in a chair or on the floor with your head, neck, and back straight, but not stiff.
- Put aside all thoughts of the past and the future, and stay in the present. Focus on the verse above.
- Become aware of your breathing. With every breath you take, allow your body to be filled with the Holy Spirit.
- Scan your body, starting with your feet, and work your way up, always ending with your head.
- Focus on the sensation of air moving in and out of your body as you breathe. Release all your sin as you exhale and invite all of God's Spirit as you inhale.
- Pay attention to the way each breath changes and is different.

L.E.A.P. 27

- Watch every thought of sin, worry, fear, anxiety, or hate come into your mind, and release it with every exhale.
- When any thoughts come up in your mind, don't ignore or suppress them but simply observe them, remaining calm and collected, giving them all to the Lord.
- If you find yourself getting carried away in your thoughts, just focus back on Jesus and simply return to your breathing, inhaling the Holy Spirit with every breath.
- Remember, do not be hard on yourself when you lose focus. You are just beginning a pure form of godly meditation.
- Now as the time comes to a close, sit for a minute or two, becoming aware of where you are, and get up gradually.

IMMANUEL

Body

L.E.A.P 27 Daily Workout Log

Date (Day/Month/Year): _____

Start Time: _____

End Time: _____

Scale Weight:	
Body Fat %:	
Fitness Goal:	Strength/Muscle Building/Fat Loss/Endurance/Other:

Body Parts Trained (Circle all that apply):

Whole Body | Chest | Back | Shoulders | Legs | Calves | Biceps | Triceps | Abs | Other: _____

CARDIO/AEROBIC/CONDITIONING EXERCISE

EXERCISE	TIME	DISTANCE/INTENSITY

WEIGHT, STRENGTH & RESISTANCE TRAINING

EXERCISE	WEIGHT	SETS	REPS	REST	NOTES

DIET & NUTRITION

MEAL	FOODS EATEN	APPROXIMATE CALORIES
BREAKFAST:		
LUNCH:		
DINNER:		

SELF EVALUATION

OVERALL WORKOUT RATING (1-10)		IMPROVEMENT NOTES:	

Day 15

THE BIRTH AND RECOGNITION OF SIN

Daily Verse

To the person who pleases him, God gives wisdom, knowledge and happiness, but to the sinner he gives the task of gathering and storing up wealth to hand it over to the one who pleases God. This too is meaningless, a chasing after the wind. (Ecclesiastes 2:26, NIV)

Now the serpent was more crafty than any of the wild animals the Lord God had made. He said to the woman, "Did God really say, 'You must not eat from any tree in the garden'?" The woman said to the serpent, "We may eat fruit from the trees in the garden, but God did say, 'You must not eat fruit from the tree that is in the middle of the garden, and you must not touch it, or you will die.'" "You will not certainly die," the serpent said to the woman. "For God knows that when you eat from it your eyes will be opened, and you will be like God, knowing good and evil." When the woman saw that the fruit of the tree was good for food and pleasing to the eye, and also desirable for gaining wisdom, she took some and ate it. She also gave some to her husband, who was with her, and he ate

IMMANUEL

it. Then the eyes of both of them were opened, and they realized they were naked; so they sewed fig leaves together and made coverings for themselves. Then the man and his wife heard the sound of the Lord God as he was walking in the garden in the cool of the day, and they hid from the Lord God among the trees of the garden. But the Lord God called to the man, "Where are you?"

He answered, "I heard you in the garden, and I was afraid because I was naked; so I hid." And he said, "Who told you that you were naked? Have you eaten from the tree that I commanded you not to eat from?" The man said, "The woman you put here with me—she gave me some fruit from the tree, and I ate it." Then the Lord God said to the woman, "What is this you have done?" The woman said, "The serpent deceived me, and I ate."

So the Lord God said to the serpent, "Because you have done this, "Cursed are you above all livestock and all wild animals! You will crawl on your belly and you will eat dust all the days of your life. And I will put enmity between you and the woman, and between your offspring and hers; he will crush your head, and you will strike his heel."

To the woman he said, "I will make your pains in childbearing very severe; with painful labor you will give birth to children. Your desire will be for your husband, and he will rule over you."

To Adam he said, "Because you listened to your wife and ate fruit from the tree about which I commanded you, 'You must not eat from it,' "Cursed is the ground because of you; through painful toil you will eat food from it all the days of your life. It will produce thorns and thistles for you, and you will eat the plants of the field. By the sweat of your brow you will eat your food until you return to the ground, since from it you were taken; for dust you are and to dust you will return."

L.E.A.P. 27

Adam named his wife Eve, because she would become the mother of all the living.

The Lord God made garments of skin for Adam and his wife and clothed them. And the Lord God said, "The man has now become like one of us, knowing good and evil. He must not be allowed to reach out his hand and take also from the tree of life and eat, and live forever." So the Lord God banished him from the Garden of Eden to work the ground from which he had been taken. After he drove the man out, he placed on the east side of the Garden of Eden cherubim and a flaming sword flashing back and forth to guard the way to the tree of life. (Genesis 3, NIV)

This was the birth of sin, and the price was death to us. Let's take a look at Genesis 3 a little closer and see how we came to fall. When the serpent (devil) saw Eve, his plan was to manipulate her into believing that the fruit was good. After their conversation, Eve looked at the fruit and saw that it was good for eating, so she took a bite and gained more wisdom than she could ever imagine. That wisdom was the difference between good and evil. Not only did she see the greatness but also she witnessed the evil that came with it. When she saw that it was good, she also offered it to Adam, in which he took it and ate it as well. They both were experiencing an overwhelming amount of wisdom that they also noticed that they were naked. They both developed feelings that they never had. They were embarrassed and ashamed. In this aspect, it's like a baby who knows nothing of this world until you teach them about it. They don't know what fear, love, anger, or jealousy are until their parents teach them. These are learned emotions that even today you still don't understand.

Then when God entered the garden and found the two, he asked them, "Who told you that you were naked?" and God knew what they had done. But he wanted to hear it from his own creation.

| 193 |

IMMANUEL

Let's take a look at the reaction that Adam and Eve gave God. God asked Adam first what had happened. Adam was the leader, and God wanted a leader's answer. But when God asked Adam about what he had done, Adam's first response was "The woman made me do it." Isn't that so interesting? One bite of the fruit, and there was no accountability for his actions, only blaming the only person he could.

When God asked Eve what had happened, her first response was just the same: "It was the serpent." She couldn't even take accountability for her own actions. She saw her partner blame her, so she was quick to blame the serpent. Doesn't that sound a lot like you and me in this present day?

When you are accused of doing something, are you quick to blame another rather than take responsibility for your own personal actions? How easy is it to just pawn it off on another? You need to change your first response, which is blaming, and focus on your second response, which is taking accountability for your own choice no matter what. Satan knows that you will blame another. That is when sin starts to build in your heart and tries to take over. When you just accept the outcome of your choice, he can't chain you up with sin.

Even though God showed Adam his punishment for disobeying his order, God still revealed much compassion for Adam and Eve. Notice the word *compassion*. He clothed them and then sent them on their way. God could have simply said, "Leave," but he didn't. What if Adam and Eve just would have told the truth about what God already knew? Would God have had compassion enough to keep them? Take a look at what accountability looks like.

Here is Job taking responsibility and not lying about it. He doesn't know what happened, but he never blamed anyone, not even God.

> We call them happy because they endured. You have heard
> of Job's patience, and you know how the Lord provided for

| 194 |

him in the end. For the Lord is full of mercy and compassion. (James 5:11, NIV)

Then Job got up and tore his clothes in grief. He shaved his head and threw himself face downward on the ground. He said, "I was born with nothing, and I will die with nothing. The lord gave, and now he has taken away. May his name be praised!" In spite of everything that had happened, Job did not sin by blaming God. (Job 1:20–22, NIV)

His wife said to him, "You are still as faithful as ever, aren't you? Why don't you curse God and die?" Job answered, "You are talking nonsense! When God sends us something good, we welcome it. How can we complain when he sends us trouble?" Even in all this suffering Job said nothing against God. (Job 2:9–10, NIV)

Job stayed faithful to God no matter what was happening in his life. But because Job stayed faithful and showed accountability for any action, even if it wasn't his fault, he was blessed with twice as much.

Then after Job had prayed for his three friends, the Lord made him prosperous again and gave him twice as much as he had before. (Job 42:10, NIV)

The Lord blessed the last part of Job's life even more than he had blessed the first. (Job 42:12, NIV)

Taking accountability for your actions will lead you to even more blessings in your life. In the next section, we will take a look at the recognition of sin: the Ten Commandments.

And God spoke all these words: "I am the Lord your God, who brought you out of Egypt, out of the land of slavery.

IMMANUEL

i. "You shall have no other gods before me.

ii. "You shall not make for yourself an image in the form of anything in heaven above or on the earth beneath or in the waters below. You shall not bow down to them or worship them; for I, the Lord your God, am a jealous God, punishing the children for the sin of the parents to the third and fourth generation of those who hate me, but showing love to a thousand generations of those who love me and keep my commandments.

iii. "You shall not misuse the name of the Lord your God, for the Lord will not hold anyone guiltless who misuses his name.

iv. "Remember the Sabbath day by keeping it holy. Six days you shall labor and do all your work, but the seventh day is a sabbath to the Lord your God. On it you shall not do any work, neither you, nor your son or daughter, nor your male or female servant, nor your animals, nor any foreigner residing in your towns. For in six days the Lord made the heavens and the earth, the sea, and all that is in them, but he rested on the seventh day. Therefore the Lord blessed the Sabbath day and made it holy.

v. "Honor your father and your mother, so that you may live long in the land the Lord your God is giving you.

vi. "You shall not murder.

vii. "You shall not commit adultery.

viii. "You shall not steal.

ix. "You shall not give false testimony against your neighbor.

x. "You shall not covet your neighbor's house. You shall not covet your neighbor's wife, or his male or female servant, his ox or donkey, or anything that belongs to your neighbor."

When the people saw the thunder and lightning and heard the trumpet and saw the mountain in smoke, they trembled with fear. They stayed at a distance and said to Moses, "Speak to us yourself and we will listen. But do not have God speak to us or we will die."

Moses said to the people, "Do not be afraid. God has come to test you, so that the fear of God will be with you to keep you from sinning." (Exodus 20:1–21, NIV)

With the Ten Commandments, we now know what sin is. These commands are not to take the fun out of life; they were made to protect your life from the trouble that God knows you can get into. We follow commands every day in school, the law, and from our parents. Before these commands were created, the people had no guidelines on how to live. How can you be held accountable if you don't know what you are doing? If your child steals something from the store yet you as a parent has never told your child that stealing is a crime, can you truly serve a punishment to fit the crime that your child had committed? Of course not. That is why you raise your children to understand the rules, not to take the fun out of life but to protect them from the trouble that they might bestow upon themselves. God is protecting you from yourself and, with his commands, assure you that if you follow them, you will be safe from harm.

> Now you must know that following all the commands are difficult in itself that is why God sent us redemption through his son Jesus Christ. The Ten Commandments is a difficult way of life but Jesus knows your hearts and when you ask for forgiveness you will be forgiven:
>
> The heart is deceitful above all things and beyond cure. Who can understand it? "I the Lord search the heart and examine the mind, to reward each person according to their conduct, according to what their deeds deserve." (Jeremiah 17:9–10, NIV)

IMMANUEL

Jesus knows your heart. You were bought with a price, and that was the sacrifice that Jesus did: to shed his blood on the cross for your sins.

Listen, my child, be wise and give serious thought to the way you live. Don't associate with people who drink too much wine or stuff themselves with food. Drunkards and gluttons will be reduced to poverty. If all you do is eat and sleep, you will soon be wearing rags. (Proverbs 23: 22–25)

LEAP Challenge 15

So today, you will acknowledge that you are not perfect, but by God's grace, you can be forgiven. If you sin today, log in your sin and pray about it by asking God for forgiveness. How do you know when you sin? The answer is taking another look at the Ten Commandments again. When you feel convicted by your sin, whether it be something small or large, you will know that the Holy Spirit is working in your life.

L.E.A.P. Insight

I finally got these words on this paper,
And now all who read it the devil is now in danger.
'Cause God's creeping through these pages as if he was the perfect stranger.
It should be distinct to everyone; God is that *clear* and *present* arranger.
You can try to give me the world, and I won't lose my soul in the process,
I was just living my life until Christ showed me the one true forgiveness.
Enemies will be everywhere I go and will be defeated even though they can't be seen,
I will never strike out when I'm up to the plate because I will always be in full swing.

| 198 |

I will be socially rejected...religiously conflicted,

I was facing two to five years, maybe even life, if I ever got convicted.

I was alcohol-addicted; the law keeping me restricted.

The pain that I caused when I was sinning in my life will never be inflicted.

So the devil will bring all his crew...and you know what I'll do...

Here you go again, swinging left to right, but with God by my side you will be subdued...

So here's a tissue...Go cry about the issue...

And make a standpoint to let the devil know you will never be spiritually abused...

Mind

Romans Chapter 15

1. T or F _____ For even Christ did not please himself but, as it is written: "The insults of those who insult you have fallen on me." (3)

   For zeal for your house consumes me, and the insults of those who insult you fall on me. (Psalm 69:9)

2. Therefore I will _____ you among the Gentiles; I will sing the _____ of your name. (9)

   Therefore I will praise you, Lord, among the nations; I will sing the praises of your name. (2 Samuel 22:50)

3. _____, you Gentiles, with his people. (10)

   Rejoice, you nations, with his people, for he will avenge the blood of his servants; he will take vengeance on his

IMMANUEL

enemies and make atonement for his land and people. (Deuteronomy 32:43)

4. _____ the Lord, all you Gentiles; let all the peoples extol him. (11)

Praise the Lord, all you nations; extol him, all you peoples. (Psalm 117:1)

5. T or F _____ Those who were not told about him will not see, and those who have not heard will not understand.

So he will sprinkle many nations, and kings will shut their mouths because of him. For what they were not told, they will see, and what they have not heard, they will understand. (Isaiah 52:15)

Mind Meditation Checklist

20 Minutes

Through love and faithfulness sin is atoned for; through the fear of the Lord evil is avoided. (Proverbs 16:6)

- Find a quiet, comfortable place. Sit in a chair or on the floor with your head, neck, and back straight, but not stiff.
- Put aside all thoughts of the past and the future, and stay in the present. Focus on the verse above.
- Become aware of your breathing. With every breath you take, allow your body to be filled with the Holy Spirit.
- Scan your body, starting with your feet, and work your way up, always ending with you head.
- Focus on the sensation of air moving in and out of your body as you breathe.

L.E.A.P. 27

- Release all your sin as you exhale, and invite all of God's Spirit as you inhale.
- Pay attention to the way each breath changes and is different.
- Watch every thought of sin, worry, fear, anxiety, or hate come into your mind, and release it with every exhale.
- When any thoughts come up in your mind, don't ignore or suppress them but simply observe them, remaining calm and collected, giving them all to the Lord.
- If you find yourself getting carried away in your thoughts, just focus back on Jesus and simply return to your breathing, inhaling the Holy Spirit with every breath.
- Remember, do not be hard on yourself when you lose focus. You are just beginning a pure form of godly meditation.
- Now as the time comes to a close, sit for a minute or two, becoming aware of where you are, and get up gradually.

IMMANUEL

Body

L.E.A.P 27 Daily Workout Log

Date (Day/Month/Year): _____

Start Time: _____

End Time: _____

Scale Weight:	
Body Fat %:	
Fitness Goal:	Strength/Muscle Building/Fat Loss/Endurance/Other:

Body Parts Trained (Circle all that apply):

Whole Body | Chest | Back | Shoulders | Legs | Calves | Biceps | Triceps | Abs | Other: _____

CARDIO/AEROBIC/CONDITIONING EXERCISE

EXERCISE	TIME	DISTANCE/INTENSITY

WEIGHT, STRENGTH & RESISTANCE TRAINING

EXERCISE	WEIGHT	SETS	REPS	REST	NOTES

DIET & NUTRITION

MEAL	FOODS EATEN	APPROXIMATE CALORIES
BREAKFAST:		
LUNCH:		
DINNER:		

SELF EVALUATION

OVERALL WORKOUT RATING (1-10)		IMPROVEMENT NOTES:	

Day 16

CONFLICT WITHIN US

Daily Verse

For the flesh desires what is contrary to the Spirit, and the Spirit what is contrary to the flesh. They are in conflict with each other, so that you are not to do whatever you want. (Galatians 5:17, NIV)

What shall we say, then? Is the law sinful? Certainly not! Nevertheless, I would not have known what sin was had it not been for the law. For I would not have known what coveting really was if the law had not said, "You shall not covet." But sin, seizing the opportunity afforded by the commandment, produced in me every kind of coveting. For apart from the law, sin was dead. Once I was alive apart from the law; but when the commandment came, sin sprang to life and I died. I found that the very commandment that was intended to bring life actually brought death. For sin, seizing the opportunity afforded by the commandment, deceived me, and through the commandment put me to death. So then, the law is holy, and the commandment is holy, righteous and good. Did that which is good, then, become death to me? By no means!

IMMANUEL

Nevertheless, in order that sin might be recognized as sin, it used what is good to bring about my death, so that through the commandment sin might become utterly sinful. We know that the law is spiritual; but I am unspiritual, sold as a slave to sin. I do not understand what I do. For what I want to do I do not do, but what I hate I do. And if I do what I do not want to do, I agree that the law is good. As it is, it is no longer I myself who do it, but it is sin living in me. For I know that good itself does not dwell in me, that is, in my sinful nature. For I have the desire to do what is good, but I cannot carry it out. For I do not do the good I want to do, but the evil I do not want to do—this I keep on doing. Now if I do what I do not want to do, it is no longer I who do it, but it is sin living in me that does it. So I find this law at work: Although I want to do good, evil is right there with me. For in my inner being I delight in God's law; but I see another law at work in me, waging war against the law of my mind and making me a prisoner of the law of sin at work within me. What a wretched man I am! Who will rescue me from this body that is subject to death? Thanks be to God, who delivers me through Jesus Christ our Lord! So then, I myself in my mind am a slave to God's law, but in my sinful nature a slave to the law of sin. (Romans 7:7–25, NIV)

In these verses, you will get the explanation that you need to know when you are struggling with your spirit and flesh. What makes this so amazing is that you are not the only one going through this. These have been going on for many centuries, and guess what? It is still going on today. You are not going through this struggle alone, so stop trying to.

What I say is this: let the Spirit direct your lives, and you will not satisfy the desires of the human nature. For what our human nature wants is opposed to what the Spirit wants, and what the Spirit wants is opposed to what our human nature wants. These two are enemies, and this means that you cannot do what you want to do. (Galatians 5:16–17, NIV)

When you need help for a math test, do you try to learn it by yourself, or do you seek the help that you need? In this same way, when you are struggling, you need to seek help through friends or family who are spiritually saved. Sometimes it's hard to ask for help in your time of need, but that is what God wants you to do. When you isolate yourself with your problems and try to figure them out alone you have to realize one important factor. You will always win no matter what. Do you understand that above statement? You are your own worst enemy and the bad thing about that is you know all your strengths and your weaknesses. You will surely use them against yourself. When God created man, he knew man would need help, so he gave man a companion.

Then the Lord God made man fall into a deep sleep, and while he was sleeping, he took out one of the man's ribs and closed up the flesh. He formed a woman out of the rib and brought her to him. Then the man said, "At last, here is one of my own kind—Bone taken from my bone, and flesh from my flesh. 'Woman' is her name because she was taken out of man." That is why a man leaves his father and mother and is united with his wife, and they become one. (Genesis 2:21–24, NIV)

The people whom you are around with when you seek support will determine your outcome. They can never make you do something that you don't want to do, but they can always influence you for the positive or negative. Remember, you don't go to a bar just to sit there and have a conversation. You go there to drink. Or you don't go to church just to take a nap. You go there to learn the message that God needs you to learn. There are many reasons why you do what you do. It is time to let God show you the reason that is a right one. Stop letting the flesh conflict with your spirit. Let the Spirit guide you on your walk.

> When they bring you to trial, do not worry about what you are going to say or how you will say it; when the time comes, you will be given what you will say. For the words you will speak will not be yours; they will come from the Spirit of your Father speaking through you. (Matthew 10:19–20, NIV)

Your spirit always wants to do what is right and speak through you, but in reality, you are made of flesh and the flesh is from this world. You can't tempt the flesh and expect the spirit to win. These are two different elements. The flesh can always be destroyed, but the Spirit lives forever.

> Do not be afraid of those who kill the body but cannot kill the soul; rather be afraid of God, who can destroy both body and soul in hell. (Matthew 10:28, NIV)

When you were saved, you now have a weapon to overcome the flesh and feed the spirit, but it is up to you. Every day, when you humble yourself before Jesus and ask for forgiveness then turn to his Word, you are strengthening your spirit. You wouldn't just get up off the couch and try to run a marathon and expect to get first place, would you? Of course not. You have to build up your body to take the pain and endurance for such a challenge. So why would you try to do the same for your spirit? You can't just pray and expect everything to go into place in your life. In the same sense for the spirit, you have to build up your spirit with prayer, meditation, and reading God's Word to take any challenge of the flesh head-on and overcome it.

Listen to your father; without him, you would not exist. When your mother is old, show her your appreciation. Truth, wisdom, learning, and good sense—these are worth paying for but are too valuable for you to sell. A righteous person's parents have good reason to be happy. You can take pride in a wise child. Let your father and mother be proud of you; give your mother that happiness. (Proverbs 23: 26–28)

LEAP Challenge 16

Building Your Spirit

1. Read God's Word (the Bible).

   > Happy is the one who reads this book, and happy are those who listen to the words of this prophetic message and obey what is written in this book! For the time is near when all these things will happen. (Revelation 1:3, NIV)

2. Meditate on what God is telling you.

   > I spend the night in deep thought; I meditate, and this is what I ask myself. (Psalms 77:6, NIV)

3. Pray, pray, pray. Oh yeah, and pray.

   > Keep watch and pray that you will not fall into temptation. The spirit is willing, but the flesh is weak. (Matthew 26:41, NIV)

Today your spirit and flesh are going to battle, and as you fight this fight, use the tools above to win this ongoing conflict. Write in your journal, and see what would be the better result: will it either be listening to your spirit or listening to your flesh? Your own happiness and stress-free life is in God's hand, and he is ready to show you the way.

IMMANUEL

L.E.A.P. Insight

Sometimes our knowledge of the things of this world cripples our ability to learn what God is trying to teach us.

Mind

Romans Chapter 16

1. Who risks their lives for Paul? (3)

_____

> There he met a Jew named Aquila, a native of Pontus, who had recently come from Italy with his wife Priscilla, because Claudius had ordered all Jews to leave Rome. (Acts 18:2)

2. T or F _____ Paul closes with a benediction, praising God and giving Him all the glory for everything. (25–27)

Mind Meditation Checklist

20 Minutes

> For we know him who said, "It is mine to avenge; I will repay," and again, "The Lord will judge his people." It is a dreadful thing to fall into the hands of the living God.
>
> Remember those earlier days after you had received the light, when you endured in a great conflict full of suffering. Sometimes you were publicly exposed to insult and persecution; at other times you stood side by side with those who were so treated. You suffered along with those in prison and joyfully accepted the confiscation of your property, because you knew that you yourselves had better

and lasting possessions. So do not throw away your confidence; it will be richly rewarded. (Hebrews 10:30–35, NIV)

- Find a quiet, comfortable place. Sit on a chair or on the floor with your head, neck, and back straight, but not stiff.
- Put aside all thoughts of the past and the future, and stay in the present. Focus on the verse above.
- Become aware of your breathing. With every breath you take, allow your body to be filled with the Holy Spirit.
- Scan your body, starting with your feet, and work your way up, always ending with your head.
- Focus on the sensation of air moving in and out of your body as you breathe. Release all your sin as you exhale, and invite all of God's Spirit as you inhale.
- Pay attention to the way each breath changes and is different.
- Watch every thought of sin, worry, fear, anxiety, or hate come into your mind, and release it with every exhale.
- When any thoughts come up in your mind, don't ignore or suppress them but simply observe them, remaining calm and collected, giving them all to the Lord.
- If you find yourself getting carried away in your thoughts, just focus back on Jesus and simply return to your breathing, inhaling the Holy Spirit with every breath.
- Remember, do not be hard on yourself when you lose focus. You are just beginning a pure form of godly meditation.
- Now as the time comes to a close, sit for a minute or two, becoming aware of where you are, and get up gradually.

IMMANUEL

Body

L.E.A.P 27 Daily Workout Log

Date (Day/Month/Year): _____

Start Time: _____

End Time: _____

Scale Weight:	
Body Fat %:	
Fitness Goal:	Strength/Muscle Building/Fat Loss/Endurance/Other:

Body Parts Trained (Circle all that apply):

Whole Body | Chest | Back | Shoulders | Legs | Calves | Biceps | Triceps | Abs | Other: _____

CARDIO/AEROBIC/CONDITIONING EXERCISE

EXERCISE	TIME	DISTANCE/INTENSITY

WEIGHT, STRENGTH & RESISTANCE TRAINING

EXERCISE	WEIGHT	SETS	REPS	REST	NOTES

DIET & NUTRITION

MEAL	FOODS EATEN	APPROXIMATE CALORIES
BREAKFAST:		
LUNCH:		
DINNER:		

SELF EVALUATION

OVERALL WORKOUT RATING (1-10)		IMPROVEMENT NOTES:	

| 210 |

Day 17

KNOWING YOUR ENEMY

Daily Verse

You are a child of the devil and an enemy of everything
that is right! You are full of all kinds of deceit and trickery.
Will you never stop perverting the right ways of the Lord?
(Acts 13:10, NIV)

"'You were the seal of perfection, full of wisdom and perfect in beauty. You were in Eden, the garden of God; every
precious stone adorned you: carnelian, chrysolite and
emerald, topaz, onyx and jasper, lapis lazuli, turquoise and
beryl. Your settings and mountings were made of gold; on
the day you were created they were prepared. You were
anointed as a guardian cherub, for so I ordained you. You
were on the holy mount of God; you walked among the
fiery stones. You were blameless in your ways from the
day you were created till wickedness was found in you.
Through your widespread trade you were filled with violence, and you sinned. So I drove you in disgrace from
the mount of God, and I expelled you, guardian cherub,
from among the fiery stones. Your heart became proud on
account of your beauty, and you corrupted your wisdom

| 211 |

because of your splendor. So I threw you to the earth; I made a spectacle of you before kings. By your many sins and dishonest trade you have desecrated your sanctuaries. So I made a fire come out from you, and it consumed you, and I reduced you to ashes on the ground in the sight of all who were watching. All the nations who knew you are appalled at you; you have come to a horrible end and will be no more.'" (Ezekiel 28:11–19, NIV)

Here you learn who the devil truly is. He is not a red beast with horns that you can see coming. You have been blinded by the evil one to look for that. But in reality, he was a fallen angel who had perfection, was full of wisdom and perfect beauty but had too much pride. He was selected to watch over the earth and be directly around God's throne in heaven. Yet before the world came to be, he became very proud, and with his wisdom, he became rebellious toward God.

Puffed up with pride, you claim to be a god. You say that like a god you sit on a throne, surrounded by the seas. You may pretend to be a god, but, no, you are mortal, not divine. You think you are wiser than Danel, that no secret can be kept from you. Your wisdom and skill make you rich with treasures of fold and silver. You made clever business deals and kept on making profits. How proud you are of your wealth! (Ezekiel 28:2–5, NIV)

When he was banished from heaven and sent to earth, he created the greatest trick ever pulled: he made the world believe he never existed. He is still doing this today. He is in our television, commercials, movies, books, magazines, the Internet, and in billboards. He has masked himself as a part of the world to hide the truth of your existence. Satan has seized a great deal of authority of the world. Here are some of the names of the devil and some inserts from the Bible so you can learn the many titles used in his description:

- God of this Age
- Kingdom of the Air
- Powers of This Dark Word
- Prince of this World
- Morning Star
- Dawn of the Day
- Satan
- Lucifer
- The Devil

> The god of this age has blinded the minds of unbelievers, so that they cannot see the light of the gospel that displays the glory of Christ, who is the image of God. (2 Corinthians 4:4, NIV)

> In which you used to live when you followed the ways of this world and of the ruler of the kingdom of the air, the spirit who is now at work in those who are disobedient. (Ephesians 2:2, NIV)

> For our struggle is not against flesh and blood, but against the rulers, against the authorities, against the powers of this dark world and against the spiritual forces of evil in the heavenly realms. (Ephesians 6:12, NIV)

> Now is the time for judgment on this world; now the prince of this world will be driven out. (John 12:31, NIV)

Now the devil has his army, which consists of a multitude of lesser angels, which are called demons. These demons are sent to help keep you blinded from the truth.

IMMANUEL

Then they brought him a demon-possessed man who was blind and mute, and Jesus healed him, so that he could both talk and see. All the people were astonished and said, "Could this be the Son of David?" But when the Pharisees heard this, they said, "It is only by Beelzebul, the prince of demons, that this fellow drives out demons." Jesus knew their thoughts and said to them, "Every kingdom divided against itself will be ruined, and every city or household divided against itself will not stand. If Satan drives out Satan, he is divided against himself. How then can his kingdom stand? And if I drive out demons by Beelzebul, by whom do your people drive them out? So then, they will be your judges. But if it is by the Spirit of God that I drive out demons, then the kingdom of God has come upon you." (Matthew 12:22–28, NIV)

"When an impure spirit comes out of a person, it goes through arid places seeking rest and does not find it. Then it says, 'I will return to the house I left.' When it arrives, it finds the house unoccupied, swept clean and put in order. Then it goes and takes with it seven other spirits more wicked than itself, and they go in and live there. And the final condition of that person is worse than the first. That is how it will be with this wicked generation." (Matthew 12:43–45, NIV)

This is a real battle going on in your life, and these are the soldiers you're up against. You have a choice in this battle. When this clash comes into play, it has influenced the world and tries to present a choice to the people. It's a choice on whether or not to follow God or the evil ways of this world. Which one will you choose? God chose you. Do you accept his choice? God will shame his enemy and make them fools.

God purposely chose what the world considers nonsense in order to shame the wise, and he chose what the world considers weak in order to shame the powerful. He chose what the world looks down on and despises and thinks is nothing, in order to destroy what the world thinks is important. This means that no one can boast in God's presence. (1 Corinthians 1:27–29, NIV)

Pay close attention, son, and let my life be your example. Prostitutes and immoral women are a deadly trap. They wait for you like robbers and cause many men to be unfaithful. (Proverbs 23: 29–35)

LEAP Challenge 17

Now that you know what you're up against, the challenge is this: separate the difference among the events that have happened to you today. Ask yourself the most important question that will help you distinguish the difference: is this situation that is going on right now from God or from the devil?

Resist all situations that lead you astray from God. One of the easiest ways to resist the devil is this: When the world tells you to do something that doesn't sound right, just do the opposite. It's just that easy.

L.E.A.P Insight

God will take vengeance on each person for their unrighteousness in becoming subject to Satan and leading astray those who dwell on the earth. We will all be like wax before the fire on that Day of Judgment, slowly melting away, and none shall be able to escape. Does this make you furious for this truthful outcome? Does this make me a man of evil feelings in my heart for saying this? No, of course not. It is because of my redemption through Christ's love that I am saying this to everyone I encounter. I am tired of sitting by watching a nation of misguided followers who truly don't know the full fledge of God's wrath. For on this day to His righteous servants, God will make a covenant for the rights to enter heaven; but for sinners, an inquisition of his judgment that shall take place according to His mercy and His patience. Now does that sound like hate? God is being merciful and patient with us so we have the opportunity to enter his glorious kingdom. Accepting a gift we don't deserve is how we all can get this, *Jesus Christ.*

Mind

Philippians Chapter 1

1. T or F _____ To all God's holy people in Christ Jesus at Philippi, together with the overseers and deacons. (1)

> From there we traveled to Philippi, a Roman colony and the leading city of that district of Macedonia. And we stayed there several days. (Acts 16:12)

2. Who is in chains for Christ? (13)

_____

> For two whole years Paul stayed there in his own rented house and welcomed all who came to see him. He proclaimed the kingdom of God and taught about the Lord Jesus Christ—with all boldness and without hindrance! (Acts 28:30)

3. T or F_____ since you (church of Philippians) are going through the same struggle you saw I had, and now hear that I still have.

When her owners realized that their hope of making money was gone, they seized Paul and Silas and dragged them into the marketplace to face the authorities. They brought them before the magistrates and said, "These men are Jews, and are throwing our city into an uproar by advocating customs unlawful for us Romans to accept or practice." The crowd joined in the attack against Paul and Silas, and the magistrates ordered them to be stripped and beaten with rods. After they had been severely flogged, they were thrown into prison, and the jailer was commanded to guard them carefully. When he received these orders, he put them in the inner cell and fastened their feet in the stocks. About midnight Paul and Silas were praying and singing hymns to God, and the other prisoners were listening to them. Suddenly there was such a violent earthquake that the foundations of the prison were shaken. At once all the prison doors flew open, and everyone's chains came loose. The jailer woke up, and when he saw the prison doors open, he drew his sword and was about to kill himself because he thought the prisoners had escaped. But Paul shouted, "Don't harm yourself! We are all here!" The jailer called for lights, rushed in and fell trembling before Paul and Silas. He then brought them out and asked, "Sirs, what must I do to be saved?" They replied, "Believe in the Lord Jesus, and you will be saved— you and your household." Then they spoke the word of the Lord to him and to all the others in his house. At that hour of the night the jailer took them and washed their wounds; then immediately he and all his household were baptized. The jailer brought them into his house and set a meal before them; he was filled with joy because he had come to believe in God—he and his whole household. When it was daylight, the magistrates sent their officers to the jailer with the order: "Release those men." The jailer told Paul, "The magistrates have ordered that you and Silas

IMMANUEL

be released. Now you can leave. Go in peace." But Paul said to the officers: "They beat us publicly without a trial, even though we are Roman citizens, and threw us into prison. And now do they want to get rid of us quietly? No! Let them come themselves and escort us out."

The officers reported this to the magistrates, and when they heard that Paul and Silas were Roman citizens, they were alarmed. They came to appease them and escorted them from the prison, requesting them to leave the city. After Paul and Silas came out of the prison, they went to Lydia's house, where they met with the brothers and sisters and encouraged them. Then they left. (Acts 16:19–40)

Mind Meditation Checklist

20 Minutes

> I will be glad and rejoice in your love, for you saw my affliction and knew the anguish of my soul. You have not given me into the hands of the enemy but have set my feet in a spacious place. (Psalm 31:7–8, NIV)

- Find a quiet, comfortable place. Sit in a chair or on the floor with your head, neck, and back straight, but not stiff.
- Put aside all thoughts of the past and the future, and stay in the present. Focus on the verse above.
- Become aware of your breathing. With every breath you take, allow your body to be filled with the Holy Spirit.
- Scan your body, starting with your feet, and work your way up, always ending with your head.
- Focus on the sensation of air moving in and out of your body as you breathe. Release all your sin as you exhale, and invite all of God's Spirit as you inhale.
- Pay attention to the way each breath changes and is different.

L.E.A.P. 27

- Watch every thought of sin, worry, fear, anxiety, or hate come into your mind, and release it with every exhale.
- When any thoughts come up in your mind, don't ignore or suppress them but simply observe them, remaining calm and collected, giving them all to the Lord.
- If you find yourself getting carried away in your thoughts, just focus back on Jesus and simply return to your breathing, inhaling the Holy Spirit with every breath.
- Remember, do not be hard on yourself when you lose focus. You are just beginning a pure form of godly meditation.
- Now as the time comes to a close, sit for a minute or two, becoming aware of where you are, and get up gradually.

IMMANUEL

Body

L.E.A.P 27 Daily Workout Log

Date (Day/Month/Year): _____

Start Time: _____

End Time: _____

Scale Weight:	
Body Fat %:	
Fitness Goal:	Strength/Muscle Building/Fat Loss/Endurance/Other:

Body Parts Trained (Circle all that apply):

Whole Body | Chest | Back | Shoulders | Legs | Calves | Biceps | Triceps | Abs | Other: _____

CARDIO/AEROBIC/CONDITIONING EXERCISE

EXERCISE	TIME	DISTANCE/INTENSITY

WEIGHT, STRENGTH & RESISTANCE TRAINING

EXERCISE	WEIGHT	SETS	REPS	REST	NOTES

DIET & NUTRITION

MEAL	FOODS EATEN	APPROXIMATE CALORIES
BREAKFAST:		
LUNCH:		
DINNER:		

SELF EVALUATION

OVERALL WORKOUT RATING (1-10)		IMPROVEMENT NOTES:	

Day 18

TRIALS AND TRIBULATIONS

Daily Verse

If this is so, then the Lord knows how to rescue the godly
from trials and to hold the unrighteous for punishment on
the day of judgment. (2 Peter 2:9, NIV)

Consider it pure joy, my brothers and sisters, whenever you
face trials of many kinds, because you know that the testing of your faith produces perseverance. Let perseverance
finish its work so that you may be mature and complete,
not lacking anything. If any of you lacks wisdom, you
should ask God, who gives generously to all without find-
ing fault, and it will be given to you. But when you ask, you
must believe and not doubt, because the one who doubts
is like a wave of the sea, blown and tossed by the wind.
That person should not expect to receive anything from
the Lord. Such a person is double-minded and unstable in
all they do. (James 1:2–8, NIV)

Trials are the least favorite part of your journey. Some can be
trivial, some can be catastrophic. What can you do? Bottom line
is this: you will always face trials in your everyday life. There is

IMMANUEL

no running away from it, but always know that through every trial, there is an escape. There are three major components that are always imminent in every trial. You must ask yourself three simple questions to understand what you are going through. Let's take a look at the simple breakdown to the formula.

1. Problem

   What is the problem that I am faced with today that is affecting my walk with Christ?

2. Complications

   What obstacles are being tossed at me that are trying to slow my progress in growing in Christ?

3. Solution

   What do I need to do to rectify the trial that I am going through?

It's that easy. You are faced with a problem in your everyday life. In trying to figure and resolve the problem, you will always come about obstacles. Once the obstacles have been acknowledged, you will then have the tools to solve the problem. That is how you must handle every trial that comes in before you in your walk with Christ.

> But if I drive out demons by the finger of God, then the kingdom of God has come to you. "When a strong man, fully armed, guards his own house, his possessions are safe. But when someone stronger attacks and overpowers him, he takes away the armor in which the man trusted and divides up the spoils. "He who is not with me is against me, and he who does not gather with me, scatters. "When an evil spirit comes out of a man, it goes through arid places seeking rest and does not find it. Then it says, 'I will return to the house I left.' When it arrives, it finds the house swept clean and put in order. Then it goes and takes

seven other spirits more wicked than itself, and they go in and live there. And the final condition of that man is worse than the first." (Luke 11:20–26, NIV)

Here today and for the rest of your life, you are going to go through trials and tribulations. Living a life with God is not an easy one. As a matter of fact, it is a great challenge that has an abundance of rewards. No matter how you feel when you change your life, you will always need God in your life so you can keep the old self from returning and trying to take over the new self. The passage above implies that we always try to change our lives, but with our own accord. We start to include God in our life, and once things seem to go great, we start to forget about him. A life completely reformed but lacking God's presence is extremely susceptible to being influenced by evil. Your own bad habits have lived inside you for so long that they don't have any place to go, so they want to return back to what it knows—you! Your unclean spirit leaves you alone, but with time, it wants to be back in control of your life. Remember, the position you're in today is due to your old ways. It takes putting one foot in front of the other to walk away from your past. No matter what trials come before you, all you need to do is put God in total control of your life. The temptation of your evil nature will surface, but remember the following:

If you think you are standing firm, be careful that you don't fall! No temptation has seized you except what is common to man. And God is faithful; he will not let you be tempted beyond what you can bear. But when you are tempted, he will also provide a way out so that you can stand up under it. (1 Corinthians 10:12–13, NIV)

Now just because you have accepted Christ and entered a relationship with God does not mean that you will no longer be lured back into your evil purpose. Accept your trials and tribulations as

IMMANUEL

a thank-you. Do not frown upon what is going on in your life. God has given you the tools you need to overcome your problem. You just have to look for him and stop handling the situation by yourself. A trial or tribulation is the discipline we all need to keep us on the right path. Think of it as a parent who disciplines their child when they misbehave. They don't do it because they hate their child but because they love them so very much and don't want to see their child engaging in bad habits. God is our parent, and our trials and tribulations are our own evil desires that need to be disciplined. Out of love, God stops us before we do wrong and begins to show us the right path. But like children, we too don't understand why things are happening in this manner. Only our Father (God) knows the true reason for the discipline and is protecting us from something we do not understand. You will be blessed in every trial that you complete. All you have to do is put God first and let him show you the way.

> Blessed is the man who perseveres under trial, because when he has stood the test, he will receive the crown of life that God has promised to those who love him. When tempted, no one should say, "God is tempting me." For God cannot be tempted by evil, nor does he tempt anyone; But each one is tempted when, by his own evil desire, he is dragged away and enticed. Then, after desire has conceived, it gives birth to sin, and sin, when it is full-grown, gives birth to death. (James 1:12–15, NIV)

Show me people who drink too much, who have to try out fancy drinks, and I will show you people who are miserable and sorry for themselves, always causing trouble and always complaining. Their eyes are bloodshot, and they have bruises that could have been avoided. Don't let wine tempt you, even though it is rich red, it sparkles in the cup, and it goes down smoothly. The next morning, you will feel as if you had been bitten by a poisonous snake. Weird sights will appear before your eyes, and you will not be able to think or speak clearly. You will feel as if you were out on the ocean, seasick, swinging high up in the rigging of a tossing ship. "I must have been hit," you will say. "I must have been beaten up, but I don't remember it. Why can't I wake up? I need another drink." (Proverbs 24: 1–2)

LEAP Challenge 18

Today, when you are faced with a trial or tribulation in your life, turn to God's Word. The Bible is your ultimate tool to defeat any trials that come your way. After you read the Bible, fall to your knees and pray to God. He is waiting for your call and ready to give you the answer you need to hear!

L.E.A.P. Insight

Somewhere along the way, you stop and realize the trials and tribulations you've experienced—every heartache you've felt, every person that let you down. You've suffered so much to the point of giving up and surrendering any hope of ever trusting anyone. But you know what? You're okay. You managed to get yourself out of bed every morning and go to work, to just live through the day. Be proud of yourself, for taking a beating and getting kicked while on the ground. Because the most important thing is you've dusted yourself and you're back on your feet. And when you think back to the toughest event of your life, you could say to yourself I've managed to live through that and no matter what I'm going through, nobody and nothing can break me because I have God with me!

Mind

Philippians Chapter 2

1. That at the name of _____ every knee should bow, in heaven and on earth and under the earth, and every tongue acknowledge that _____ is Lord, to the glory of God the Father. (10–11)

> By myself I have sworn, my mouth has uttered in all integrity a word that will not be revoked: Before me every knee will bow; by me every tongue will swear. (Isaiah 45:23)

2. T or F _____ God wants his children without fault in a warped and crooked generation. (15)

> They are corrupt and not his children; to their shame they are a warped and crooked generation. (Deuteronomy 32:5)

Mind Meditation Checklist

20 Minutes

> For that righteous man, living among them day after day, was tormented in his righteous soul by the lawless deeds he saw and heard)—if this is so, then the Lord knows how to rescue the godly from trials and to hold the unrighteous for punishment on the day of judgment. This is especially true of those who follow the corrupt desire of the flesh and despise authority. (2 Peter 2:8–10, NIV)

- Find a quiet, comfortable place. Sit in a chair or on the floor with your head, neck, and back straight, but not stiff.

L.E.A.P. 27

- Put aside all thoughts of the past and the future, and stay in the present. Focus on the verse above.
- Become aware of your breathing. With every breath you take, allow your body to be filled with the Holy Spirit.
- Scan your body, starting with your feet, and work your way up, always ending with your head.
- Focus on the sensation of air moving in and out of your body as you breathe. Release all your sin as you exhale, and invite all of God's Spirit as you inhale.
- Pay attention to the way each breath changes and is different.
- Watch every thought of sin, worry, fear, anxiety, or hate come into your mind, and release it with every exhale.
- When any thoughts come up in your mind, don't ignore or suppress them but simply observe them, remaining calm and collected, giving them all to the Lord.
- If you find yourself getting carried away in your thoughts, just focus back on Jesus and simply return to your breathing, inhaling the Holy Spirit with every breath.
- Remember, do not be hard on yourself when you lose focus. You are just beginning a pure form of godly meditation.
- Now as the time comes to a close, sit for a minute or two, becoming aware of where you are, and get up gradually.

IMMANUEL

Body

L.E.A.P 27 Daily Workout Log

Date (Day/Month/Year): _____

Start Time: _____

End Time: _____

Scale Weight:	
Body Fat %:	
Fitness Goal:	Strength/Muscle Building/Fat Loss/Endurance/Other:

Body Parts Trained (Circle all that apply):

Whole Body | Chest | Back | Shoulders | Legs | Calves | Biceps | Triceps | Abs | Other: _____

CARDIO/AEROBIC/CONDITIONING EXERCISE

EXERCISE	*TIME*	*DISTANCE/INTENSITY*

WEIGHT, STRENGTH & RESISTANCE TRAINING

EXERCISE	*WEIGHT*	*SETS*	*REPS*	*REST*	*NOTES*

DIET & NUTRITION

MEAL	*FOODS EATEN*	*APPROXIMATE CALORIES*
BREAKFAST:		
LUNCH:		
DINNER:		

SELF EVALUATION

OVERALL WORKOUT RATING (1-10)		IMPROVEMENT NOTES:	

Day 19

SATAN'S FALL

Daily Verse

But there were also false prophets among the people, just as there will be false teachers among you. They will secretly introduce destructive heresies, even denying the sovereign Lord who bought them—bringing swift destruction on themselves. Many will follow their depraved conduct and will bring the way of truth into disrepute. In their greed these teachers will exploit you with fabricated stories. Their condemnation has long been hanging over them, and their destruction has not been sleeping. (2 Peter 2:1–3, NIV)

On the day the Lord gives you relief from your suffering and turmoil and from the harsh labor forced on you, you will take up this taunt against the king of Babylon:
How the oppressor has come to an end! How his fury has ended! The Lord has broken the rod of the wicked, the scepter of the rulers, which in anger struck down peoples with unceasing blows, and in fury subdued nations with relentless aggression. All the lands are at rest and at peace; they break into singing. Even the junipers and the cedars of Lebanon gloat over you and say, "Now that you have

| 229 |

IMMANUEL

been laid low, no one comes to cut us down." The realm of the dead below is all astir to meet you at your coming; it rouses the spirits of the departed to greet you—all those who were leaders in the world; it makes them rise from their thrones—all those who were kings over the nations. They will all respond, they will say to you, "You also have become weak, as we are; you have become like us." All your pomp has been brought down to the grave, along with the noise of your harps; maggots are spread out beneath you and worms cover you. How you have fallen from heaven, morning star, son of the dawn! You have been cast down to the earth, you who once laid low the nations! You said in your heart, "I will ascend to the heavens; I will raise my throne above the stars of God; I will sit enthroned on the mount of assembly, on the utmost heights of Mount Zaphon. I will ascend above the tops of the clouds; I will make myself like the Most High." But you are brought down to the realm of the dead, to the depths of the pit. Those who see you stare at you, they ponder your fate: "Is this the man who shook the earth and made kingdoms tremble, the man who made the world a wilderness, who overthrew its cities and would not let his captives go home?" All the kings of the nations lie in state, each in his own tomb. But you are cast out of your tomb like a rejected branch; you are covered with the slain, with those pierced by the sword, those who descend to the stones of the pit. Like a corpse trampled underfoot, you will not join them in burial, for you have destroyed your land and killed your people. (Isaiah 14:3–20, NIV)

In Isaiah 14, we learn that the fall will happen to the devil due to his prideful, rebellious behavior toward God and is thrown out of heaven. This may be his world in which he has manipulated, but he has no control on the believers of God in heaven.

> When the thousand years are over, Satan will be released from his prison and will go out to deceive the nations in the four corners of the earth—Gog and Magog—and to gather them for battle. In number they are like the sand on the seashore. They marched across the breadth of the earth and surrounded the camp of God's people, the city he loves. But fire came down from heaven and devoured them. And the devil, who deceived them, was thrown into the lake of burning sulfur, where the beast and the false prophet had been thrown. They will be tormented day and night for ever and ever. (Revelations 20:7–10, NIV)

In Revelations 20, it states that Satan will be released to deceive the nations of the world. This will be the last rebellion against God forever. Does this sound familiar? Is this world truly betraying you?

During this time, you will have a choice to make: are you with the God of truth or are you with the devil of lies? It is human nature to be deceived by the devil, so don't be complacent with your walk with God. At the end of the devil's reign, he will be thrown into the lake of fire. After Satan's fall, there will be one final judgment for us all:

> Then I saw a great white throne and him who was seated on it. The earth and the heavens fled from his presence, and there was no place for them. And I saw the dead, great and small, standing before the throne, and books were opened. Another book was opened, which is the book of life. The dead were judged according to what they had done as recorded in the books. The sea gave up the dead that were in it, and death and Hades gave up the dead that were in them, and each person was judged according to what they had done. Then death and Hades were thrown into the lake of fire. The lake of fire is the second death. Anyone

whose name was not found written in the book of life was thrown into the lake of fire. (Revelations 20:11–15, NIV)

This is the final judgment of God and according to what you have done in this world will be recorded in the book of life. Every selfish and defiant act will be called into account. For the lives that did not accept God's forgiveness, which is Jesus Christ, will be thrown in the lake of fire.

"You were like a ship at sea loaded with heavy cargo. When your oarsmen brought you out to sea, An east wind wrecked you far from land. All your wealth of merchandise, all the sailors in your crew, your ship's carpenters and your merchants, every soldier on board the ship—all, all were lost at sea when your ship was wrecked. The shouts of the drowning sailors echoed on the shore. "Every ship is now deserted, and every sailor has gone ashore. They all mourn bitterly for you, throwing dust on their heads and rolling in ashes. They shave their heads for you and dress themselves in sackcloth. Their hearts are bitter as they weep. They chant a funeral song for you: 'Who can be compared to Tyre, to Tyre now silent in the sea? When your merchandise went overseas, you filled the needs of every nation. Kings were made rich by the wealth of your goods. Now you are wrecked in the sea; you have sunk to the ocean depths. Your goods and all who worked for you have vanished with you in the sea.'

"Everyone who lives along the coast is shocked at your fate. Even their kings are terrified, and fear is written on their faces. You are gone, gone forever, and merchants all over the world are terrified, afraid that they will share your fate." (Ezekiel 27:25–36, NIV)

Satan will be buried with his deceptive minions and false prophets. And every mortal man will sing his funeral song. Do you notice how every worldly object will sink down with him? And mortal men and women will cry for them. Are your priorities straight, or are you stuck on worldly things?

So the question to ask yourself is this: do you want to make your life easy? All God asks is for you to accept his Son, Jesus Christ, into your life. This is the gift of God's salvation for you.

> For God did not send his Son into the world to condemn the world, but to save the world through him. (John 3:17, NIV)

Don't be envious of evil people, and don't try to make friends with them. Causing trouble is all they ever think about; every time they open their mouth someone is going to be hurt. (Proverbs 24: 3-4)

LEAP Challenge 19

Today you will see the deception of the devil firsthand. On your everyday walk, take a look at everything around you and ask yourself, Do I really need all the things this world has to offer?

L.E.A.P Insight

The myth of man we will all become, from the devil's deception that we will succumb. Lack of knowledge will render our very soul; due to the social media's total loss of control. So wise up, all God's people who will surrender the call, and don't become a statistic in Satan's great fall.

1. Do you really need that new car in the showroom?
2. Do you really need all the makeup products they have to offer?
3. Do my kids really need all the toys that are displayed on TV?

IMMANUEL

4. How graphic is regular television compared to twenty years ago?
5. Are you getting a $140,000 salary by watching football, basketball, or baseball that you can't miss the game?

You are reborn, and Satan's fall will not be yours. Do not cry over worldly objects. Instead, praise God when something is taken from you. Only then will he know that you are truly satisfied with his love.

Mind

Philippians Chapter 3

1. T or F _____ We who serve God by his Spirit, who boast in Christ Jesus, and who put no confidence in the flesh. (3)

   But he said to me, "My grace is sufficient for you, for my power is made perfect in weakness." Therefore I will boast all the more gladly about my weaknesses, so that Christ's power may rest on me. (2 Corinthians 12:9)

2. I want to know Christ—yes, to know the power of his _____ and participation in his sufferings, becoming like him in his death, and so, somehow, attaining to the _____ from the dead. (10–11)

   They were greatly disturbed because the apostles were teaching the people, proclaiming in Jesus the resurrection of the dead. (Acts 4:2)

Mind Meditation Checklist

20 Minutes

> "All this I will give you," he said, "if you will bow down and worship me."
>
> Jesus said to him, "Away from me, Satan! For it is written: 'Worship the Lord your God, and serve him only.'" Then the devil left him, and angels came and attended him. (Matthew 4:9–11, NIV)

- Find a quiet, comfortable place. Sit in a chair or on the floor with your head, neck, and back straight, but not stiff.
- Put aside all thoughts of the past and the future, and stay in the present. Focus on the verse above.
- Become aware of your breathing. With every breath you take, allow your body to be filled with the Holy Spirit.
- Scan your body, starting with your feet, and work your way up, always ending with your head.
- Focus on the sensation of air moving in and out of your body as you breathe. Release all your sin as you exhale, and invite all of God's Spirit as you inhale.
- Pay attention to the way each breath changes and is different.
- Watch every thought of sin, worry, fear, anxiety, or hate come into your mind, and release it with every exhale.
- When any thoughts come up in your mind, don't ignore or suppress them but simply observe them, remaining calm and collected, giving them all to the Lord.
- If you find yourself getting carried away in your thoughts, just focus back on Jesus and simply return to your breathing, inhaling the Holy Spirit with every breath.
- Remember, do not be hard on yourself when you lose focus. You are just beginning a pure form of godly meditation.
- Now as the time comes to a close, sit for a minute or two, becoming aware of where you are, and get up gradually.

IMMANUEL

Body

L.E.A.P 27 Daily Workout Log

Date (Day/Month/Year): _____

Start Time: _____

End Time: _____

Scale Weight:	
Body Fat %:	
Fitness Goal:	Strength/Muscle Building/Fat Loss/Endurance/Other:

Body Parts Trained (Circle all that apply):

Whole Body | Chest | Back | Shoulders | Legs | Calves | Biceps | Triceps | Abs | Other: _____

CARDIO/AEROBIC/CONDITIONING EXERCISE

EXERCISE	TIME	DISTANCE/INTENSITY

WEIGHT, STRENGTH & RESISTANCE TRAINING

EXERCISE	WEIGHT	SETS	REPS	REST	NOTES

DIET & NUTRITION

MEAL	FOODS EATEN	APPROXIMATE CALORIES
BREAKFAST:		
LUNCH:		
DINNER:		

SELF EVALUATION

OVERALL WORKOUT RATING (1-10)		IMPROVEMENT NOTES:	

Day 20

WORLD VIEWS

Daily Verse

What good will it be for someone to gain the whole world, yet forfeit their soul? Or what can anyone give in exchange for their soul? (Matthew 16:26, NIV)

What causes fights and quarrels among you? Don't they come from your desires that battle within you? You desire but do not have, so you kill. You covet but you cannot get what you want, so you quarrel and fight. You do not have because you do not ask God. When you ask, you do not receive, because you ask with wrong motives, that you may spend what you get on your pleasures. You adulterous people, don't you know that friendship with the world means enmity against God? Therefore, anyone who chooses to be a friend of the world becomes an enemy of God. Or do you think Scripture says without reason that he jealously longs for the spirit he has caused to dwell in us? But he gives us more grace. That is why Scripture says:

"God opposes the proud but shows favor to the humble."

Submit yourselves, then, to God. Resist the devil, and he will flee from you. Come near to God and he will come

IMMANUEL

near to you. Wash your hands, you sinners, and purify your hearts, you double-minded. Grieve, mourn and wail. Change your laughter to mourning and your joy to gloom. Humble yourselves before the Lord, and he will lift you up. Brothers and sisters, do not slander one another. Anyone who speaks against a brother or sister or judges them speaks against the law and judges it. When you judge the law, you are not keeping it, but sitting in judgment on it. There is only one Lawgiver and Judge, the one who is able to save and destroy. But you—who are you to judge your neighbor? (James 4:1–10, NIV))

This is a time to stay strong as well as humble yourself toward God. The world will not understand how different you are; be very careful not to fall back onto the world views. You are now living a spiritual life through soul, body, and mind. You are seeing the world with your eyes wide open, and God is showing you what the world has become. This is the same world that, just twenty days ago, told you that you're not beautiful enough, rich enough, smart enough, you don't have a nice car, you are alone in this world, and you don't have a great spouse or family, so just drown your pain in drugs and alcohol. Yes, this is still that same world.

As for you, you were dead in your transgressions and sins, in which you used to live when you followed the ways of this world and of the ruler of the kingdom of the air, the spirit who is now at work in those who are disobedient. All of us also lived among them at one time, gratifying the cravings of our flesh and following its desires and thoughts.

Like the rest, we were by nature deserving of wrath. But because of his great love for us, God, who is rich in mercy, made us alive with Christ even when we were dead in transgressions—it is by grace you have been saved. (Ephesians 2:1–5, NIV)

L.E.A.P. 27

> You were at one time spiritually dead because of your sins and because you were Gentiles without the Law. But God has now brought you to life with Christ. (Colossians 2:13, NIV)

These are things that work like a huge curtain, just hiding the truth from you. This truth is simple that no matter how much you have in your life; your flesh will always want more. The more the flesh is feed the more problems you will endure. You can never please the flesh, but you can always delight the spirit. In reality God has made you to have a simple purpose, but your flesh is the one that complicates the situation. Your flesh wants to devour the resources that life has to offer, while the spirit wishes to nourish it.

> Lo, this only have I found, that God hath made man upright; but they have sought out many inventions. (Ecclesiastes 7:29, KJV)

Remember what Jesus said: "Seek and you shall find; knock and the door will be opened; ask and you shall receive." This saying works both ways. What you seek, knock, or ask for shall be given, either good or bad. Be careful what you search for in your life.

> If you believe, you will receive whatever you ask for in prayer. (Matthew 21:22, NIV)

> But I know that even now God will give you whatever you ask him for. (John 11:22, NIV)

Don't let this world try to mask who you truly are, which is God's children; you're loved, blessed, saved, accepted, understood, made for a purpose, and special. The world will not understand why you are receiving so many blessings and will become envi-

| 239 |

IMMANUEL

ous of you. Always stay humble. And never forget that if you don't get something right away or even at all; there is always a reason. What you may consider a blessing could actually be your demise into failure. Only God truly knows and will never allow you to fail.

> "If the world hates you, keep in mind that it hated me first. If you belonged to the world, it would love you as its own. As it is, you do not belong to the world, but I have chosen you out of the world. That is why the world hates you. Remember what I told you: 'A servant is not greater than his master.' If they persecuted me, they will persecute you also. If they obeyed my teaching, they will obey yours also. They will treat you this way because of my name, for they do not know the one who sent me. If I had not come and spoken to them, they would not be guilty of sin; but now they have no excuse for their sin. Whoever hates me hates my Father as well. If I had not done among them the works no one else did, they would not be guilty of sin. As it is, they have seen, and yet they have hated both me and my Father. But this is to fulfill what is written in their Law: 'They hated me without reason.' (John 15:18–27, NIV)

Do not fall short of God's glory and grace. Stay strong in his Word, and pray and meditate every day. In the end, the world will crumble and the views of this world will try to overtake God's people. As long as you stay in God's Word (the Bible), which is the truth, the world views and lies cannot overtake your spirit that God has sent to you.

> But mark this: There will be terrible times in the last days. People will be lovers of themselves, lovers of money, boastful, proud, abusive, disobedient to their parents, ungrateful, unholy, without love, unforgiving, slanderous, without self–control, brutal, not lovers of the good, treacherous,

rash, conceited, lovers of pleasure rather than lovers of God—having a form of godliness but denying its power. Have nothing to do with such people. They are the kind who worm their way into homes and gain control over gullible women, who are loaded down with sins and are swayed by all kinds of evil desires, always learning but never able to come to a knowledge of the truth. Just as Jannes and Jambres opposed Moses, so also these teachers oppose the truth. They are men of depraved minds, who, as far as the faith is concerned, are rejected. But they will not get very far because, as in the case of those men, their folly will be clear to everyone. (2 Timothy 3:1–9, NIV)

You have to recognize the fact that you live in a battle of complexity, with a strategic plan of simplicity: Jesus Christ.

Homes are built on the foundation of wisdom and understanding. Where there is knowledge, the rooms are furnished with valuable beautiful things. (Proverbs 24: 5–6)

LEAP Challenge 20

It is time to make two lists, one with all that God has given you and another with all that you have received for the flesh. On that list, describe some of the emotional feelings that you endured. Ask yourself these few questions:

- Was it positive or negative?
- Does this help my spiritual walk?
- Is this keeping me from my true reason on why I'm here?
- Am I using it to help others?

L.E.A.P. Insight

Being a part of a comprehensive world view (or worldview) is the fundamental cognitive orientation of you as an individual or

IMMANUEL

part of a society encompassing the entirety of the individual or society's knowledge and point of view. When you choose to follow this world's view point, you would fall into a category called a cult. If you don't agree, take a close look at our world "cult"ure.

Mind

Philippians Chapter 4

1. Which city shared with Paul in the matter of giving and receiving? (15)

_____

> And when I was with you and needed something, I was not a burden to anyone, for the brothers who came from Macedonia supplied what I needed. I have kept myself from being a burden to you in any way, and will continue to do so. (2 Corinthians 11:9)

Mind Meditation Checklist

20 Minutes

> My prayer is not that you take them out of the world but that you protect them from the evil one. They are not of the world, even as I am not of it. Sanctify them by the truth; your word is truth. (John 17:15–17, NIV)

- Find a quiet, comfortable place. Sit in a chair or on the floor with your head, neck, and back straight, but not stiff.
- Put aside all thoughts of the past and the future, and stay in the present. Focus on the verse above.
- Become aware of your breathing. With every breath you take, allow your body to be filled with the Holy Spirit.

L.E.A.P. 27

- Scan your body, starting with your feet, and work your way up, always ending with your head.
- Focus on the sensation of air moving in and out of your body as you breathe. Release all your sin as you exhale, and invite all of God's Spirit as you inhale.
- Pay attention to the way each breath changes and is different.
- Watch every thought of sin, worry, fear, anxiety, or hate come into your mind, and release it with every exhale.
- When any thoughts come up in your mind, don't ignore or suppress them but simply observe them, remaining calm and collected, giving them all to the Lord.
- If you find yourself getting carried away in your thoughts, just focus back on Jesus and simply return to your breathing, inhaling the Holy Spirit with every breath.
- Remember, do not be hard on yourself when you lose focus. You are just beginning a pure form of godly meditation.
- Now as the time comes to a close, sit for a minute or two, becoming aware of where you are, and get up gradually.

IMMANUEL

Body

L.E.A.P 27 Daily Workout Log

Date (Day/Month/Year): _____

Start Time: _____

End Time: _____

Scale Weight:	
Body Fat %:	
Fitness Goal:	Strength/Muscle Building/Fat Loss/Endurance/Other:

Body Parts Trained (Circle all that apply):

Whole Body | Chest | Back | Shoulders | Legs | Calves | Biceps | Triceps | Abs | Other: _____

CARDIO/AEROBIC/CONDITIONING EXERCISE

EXERCISE	TIME	DISTANCE/INTENSITY

WEIGHT, STRENGTH & RESISTANCE TRAINING

EXERCISE	WEIGHT	SETS	REPS	REST	NOTES

DIET & NUTRITION

MEAL	FOODS EATEN	APPROXIMATE CALORIES
BREAKFAST:		
LUNCH:		
DINNER:		

SELF EVALUATION

OVERALL WORKOUT RATING (1-10)		IMPROVEMENT NOTES:	

Day 21

GOD GIVES

Daily Verse

> So give me the wisdom and knowledge I need to rule over them. Otherwise, how would I ever be able to rule this great people of yours? (2 Chronicles 1:10, NIV)

> If the Spirit of God, who raised Jesus from death, lives in you, then he who raised Christ from death will also give life to your mortal bodies by the presence of his Spirit in you. (Romans 8:11, NIV)

God has given you one of the greatest gifts. Notice that when you accepted Christ in your life, the Spirit of God that raised Jesus from death gives life in your mortal body. You have such a powerful gift just lying dormant inside you, just waiting to come out.

> Trust in the Lord and do good; live in the land and be safe. Seek your happiness in the Lord, and he will give you your heart's desire. (Psalms 37:3–4, NIV)

Take a look at what the above verse is asking of you. Seek your happiness in Jesus, and you will receive what your heart

IMMANUEL

desires. God has been giving you many gifts all along; you just didn't know how to accept them. How can I seek the happiness of Christ?

> And now I give you a new commandment: love one another. As I loved you, so you must love one another. (John 13:34, NIV)

It all starts with love. The happiness of Christ lies in love for one another. Now that you have what God has given you, it is time for you to share the gift with others who need it. You must give the most important gift that God gave you and share it with others.

> But Peter said to him, "I have no money at all, but I give you what I have: in the name of Jesus Christ of Nazareth I order you to get up and walk!" (Acts 3:6, NIV)

> Each one should give, then as he has decided, not with regret or out of a sense of duty; for God loves the one who gives more than you need, so that you will always have all you need for yourselves and more than enough for every good cause. (2 Corinthians 9:7–8, NIV)

> But the Grace that God gives is even stronger. As the scripture says, "God resists the proud, but gives grace to the humble." (James 4:6, NIV)

Being wise is better than being strong; yes, knowledge is more important than strength. After all, you must make careful plans before you fight a battle, and the more good advice you get, the more likely you are to win. (Proverbs 24: 7)

LEAP Challenge 21

Today you will learn to accept the gift that God is giving you. Make sure you take a close look at what God is giving you on this glorious day. Always remember, whatever God gives you is a gift, and even though you sometimes feel like you don't deserve it, learn to just accept it.

L.E.A.P. Insight

"You give but little when you give of your possessions. It is when you give of yourself that you truly give."

—Kahlil Gibran

Mind

Today is a free day from answering questions. Enjoy today, and keep your mind preoccupied for the day. You can do one of these choices on the list below:

- Read a book.
- Do a puzzle.
- Work on a crossword puzzle.
- Do Sudoku.
- Read the newspaper.

You get the idea. Well, you have a blessed day today.

Mind Meditation Checklist

20 Minutes

May he remember all your sacrifices and accept your burnt offerings. May he give you the desire of your heart

IMMANUEL

and make all your plans succeed. May we shout for joy over your victory and lift up our banners in the name of our God. May the Lord grant all your requests. (Psalm 20:3–5, NIV)

- Find a quiet, comfortable place. Sit in a chair or on the floor with your head, neck, and back straight, but not stiff.
- Put aside all thoughts of the past and the future, and stay in the present. Focus on the verse above.
- Become aware of your breathing. With every breath you take, allow your body to be filled with the Holy Spirit.
- Scan your body, starting with your feet, and work your way up, always ending with your head.
- Focus on the sensation of air moving in and out of your body as you breathe. Release all your sin as you exhale, and invite all of God's Spirit as you inhale.
- Pay attention to the way each breath changes and is different.
- Watch every thought of sin, worry, fear, anxiety, or hate come into your mind, and release it with every exhale.
- When any thoughts come up in your mind, don't ignore or suppress them but simply observe them, remaining calm and collected, giving them all to the Lord.
- If you find yourself getting carried away in your thoughts, just focus back on Jesus and simply return to your breathing, inhaling the Holy Spirit with every breath.
- Remember, do not be hard on yourself when you lose focus. You are just beginning a pure form of godly meditation.
- Now as the time comes to a close, sit for a minute or two, becoming aware of where you are, and get up gradually.

Body

L.E.A.P 27 Daily Workout Log

Date (Day/Month/Year): _____

Start Time: _____

End Time: _____

Scale Weight:	
Body Fat %:	
Fitness Goal:	Strength/Muscle Building/Fat Loss/Endurance/Other:

Body Parts Trained (Circle all that apply):

Whole Body | Chest | Back | Shoulders | Legs | Calves | Biceps | Triceps | Abs | Other: _____

CARDIO/AEROBIC/CONDITIONING EXERCISE

EXERCISE	TIME	DISTANCE/INTENSITY

WEIGHT, STRENGTH & RESISTANCE TRAINING

EXERCISE	WEIGHT	SETS	REPS	REST	NOTES

DIET & NUTRITION

MEAL	FOODS EATEN	APPROXIMATE CALORIES
BREAKFAST:		
LUNCH:		
DINNER:		

SELF EVALUATION

OVERALL WORKOUT RATING (1-10)		IMPROVEMENT NOTES:	

Day 22

GOD'S PLAN

Daily Verse

"For I know the plans I have for you," says the Lord. "They are plans for good and not for disaster, to give you a future and a hope." (Jeremiah 29:11, NIV)

His divine power has given us everything we need for a godly life through our knowledge of him who called us by his own glory and goodness. Through these he has given us his very great and precious promises, so that through them you may participate in the divine nature, having escaped the corruption in the world caused by evil desires. For this very reason, make every effort to add to your faith goodness; and to goodness, knowledge; and to knowledge, self-control; and to self-control, perseverance; and to perseverance, godliness; and to godliness, mutual affection; and to mutual affection, love. For if you possess these qualities in increasing measure, they will keep you from being ineffective and unproductive in your knowledge of our Lord Jesus Christ. But whoever does not have them is nearsighted and blind, forgetting that they have been cleansed from

IMMANUEL

their past sins. Therefore, my brothers and sisters, make every effort to confirm your calling and election. For if you do these things, you will never stumble, and you will receive a rich welcome into the eternal kingdom of our Lord and Savior Jesus Christ. (2 Peter 1:3–11, NIV)

God has given you a documented plan to live by so you can organize your own calling in life. You will take a closer look at God's divine blueprint so you can share it with others. First, let us add a name to your effort of this plan. That name is Jesus.

1. Increase your faith with Jesus' goodness. Now your goodness is unbreakable.
2. Your unbreakable goodness with Jesus's knowledge. Now your knowledge is unthinkable.
3. Your unthinkable knowledge with Jesus's self-control. Now your self-control is indescribable.
4. Your indescribable self-control with Jesus's steadfastness (dedication). Now your steadfastness is uncontrollable.
5. Your uncontrollable steadfastness with Jesus's godliness. Now your godliness is inexpressible.
6. Your inexpressible godliness with Jesus's affection. Now your affection is powerful.
7. Your powerful affection with Jesus's love. Now your love is unforgettable.

If you live in this manner every day, you have now become an unbreakable, unimaginable, indescribable, uncontrollable, inexpressible, powerful, and unforgettable soldier in God's army. These are some powerful attributes that you have in your life all by the faith in Jesus Christ. This is God's plan that was made for you even before you were born. Now go and take a look in the mirror today so you can stare at what he has created. Cherish what you see because you are special in your Creator's eyes. It's time for you to believe too.

God is our shelter and strength, always ready to help in times of trouble. So we will not be afraid, even if the earth is shaken and mountains fall into the ocean depths; even if the seas roar and rage, and the hills are shaken by the violence. There is a river that brings joy to the city of God, to the sacred house of the Most High. God is in that city, and it will never be destroyed; at early dawn he will come to its aid. Nations are terrified, kingdoms are shaken; God thunders, and the earth dissolves. The Lord Almighty is with us; the God of Jacob is our refuge. Come and see what the Lord has done. See what amazing things he has done on earth. He stops wars all over the world; he breaks bows, destroys spears, and sets shields on fire. "Stop fighting," he says, "and know that I am God, supreme among the nations, supreme over the world." The Lord Almighty is with us; The God of Jacob is our refuge. (Psalms 46, NIV)

God's plan is very simple. He will conquer this world and take his people with him. Are you ready to be with the Lord Almighty?

Wise sayings are too deep for a stupid person to understand. He has nothing to say when important matters are being discussed. (Proverbs 24: 8-9)

LEAP Challenge 22

Let's walk with Christ today. Tell yourself today, "Lord, let me be like you so the ones that I love dearly can be like me." Change your own world one person at a time. On this page, make a list of all the people that you spoke to. Help them walk in the light, as you are doing.

L.E.A.P. Insight

We need to *stop* asking God "Why do you send people to hell?" We need to *start* asking God "What can I do to prevent it?"

IMMANUEL

All of Gods people take a stand today. Speak to just one person today and be a miracle in their life. Are you up for the challenge?

Mind

1 Thessalonians Chapter 1

1. Our _____ came to you not simply with words but also with power, with the Holy Spirit and deep conviction. You know how we lived among you for your sake. (5)

> For in the gospel the righteousness of God is revealed—a righteousness that is by faith from first to last, just as it is written: "The righteous will live by faith." (Romans 1:17)

2. T or F _____ You became imitators of us and of the Lord, for you welcomed the message in the midst of severe suffering with the joy given by the Holy Spirit.

> But other Jews were jealous; so they rounded up some bad characters from the marketplace, formed a mob and started a riot in the city. They rushed to Jason's house in search of Paul and Silas in order to bring them out to the crowd. But when they did not find them, they dragged Jason and some other believers before the city officials, shouting: "These men who have caused trouble all over the world have now come here, and Jason has welcomed them into his house.
>
> They are all defying Caesar's decrees, saying that there is another king, one called Jesus." When they heard this, the crowd and the city officials were thrown into turmoil. Then they made Jason and the others post bond and let them go. (Acts 17:5–9)

| 254 |

Mind Meditation Checklist

25 Minutes

> And I, because of what they have planned and done, am about to come and gather the people of all nations and languages, and they will come and see my glory. (Isaiah 66:18, NIV)

- Find a quiet, comfortable place. Sit in a chair or on the floor with your head, neck, and back straight, but not stiff.
- Put aside all thoughts of the past and the future, and stay in the present. Focus on the verse above.
- Become aware of your breathing. With every breath you take, allow your body to be filled with the Holy Spirit.
- Scan your body, starting with your feet, and work your way up, always ending with your head.
- Focus on the sensation of air moving in and out of your body as you breathe. Release all your sin as you exhale, and invite all of God's Spirit as you inhale.
- Pay attention to the way each breath changes and is different.
- Watch every thought of sin, worry, fear, anxiety, or hate come into your mind, and release it with every exhale.
- When any thoughts come up in your mind, don't ignore or suppress them, but simply observe them, remaining calm and collected, giving them all to the Lord.
- If you find yourself getting carried away in your thoughts, just focus back on Jesus and simply return to your breathing, inhaling the Holy Spirit with every breath.
- Remember, do not be hard on yourself when you lose focus. You are just beginning a pure form of godly meditation.
- Now as the time comes to a close, sit for a minute or two, becoming aware of where you are, and get up gradually.

IMMANUEL

Body

L.E.A.P 27 Daily Workout Log

Date (Day/Month/Year): _____

Start Time: _____

End Time: _____

Scale Weight:	
Body Fat %:	
Fitness Goal:	Strength/Muscle Building/Fat Loss/Endurance/Other:

Body Parts Trained (Circle all that apply):

Whole Body | Chest | Back | Shoulders | Legs | Calves | Biceps | Triceps | Abs | Other: _____

CARDIO/AEROBIC/CONDITIONING EXERCISE

EXERCISE	TIME	DISTANCE/INTENSITY

WEIGHT, STRENGTH & RESISTANCE TRAINING

EXERCISE	WEIGHT	SETS	REPS	REST	NOTES

DIET & NUTRITION

MEAL	FOODS EATEN	APPROXIMATE CALORIES
BREAKFAST:		
LUNCH:		
DINNER:		

SELF EVALUATION

OVERALL WORKOUT RATING (1-10)		IMPROVEMENT NOTES:	

Day 23

GOD'S PROMISE

Daily Verse

The promise is for you and your children and for all who are far off—for all whom the Lord our God will call. (Acts 2:39, NIV)

Now when Jesus saw the crowds, he went up on a mountainside and sat down. His disciples came to him, and he began to teach them. He said:

"Blessed are the poor in spirit, for theirs is the kingdom of heaven.

Blessed are those who mourn, for they will be comforted.

Blessed are the meek, for they will inherit the earth.

Blessed are those who hunger and thirst for righteousness, for they will be filled.

Blessed are the merciful, for they will be shown mercy.

Blessed are the pure in heart, for they will see God.

Blessed are the peacemakers, for they will be called children of God.

Blessed are those who are persecuted because of righteousness, for theirs is the kingdom of heaven.

IMMANUEL

"Blessed are you when people insult you, persecute you and falsely say all kinds of evil against you because of me. Rejoice and be glad, because great is your reward in heaven, for in the same way they persecuted the prophets who were before you." (Matthew 5:1–12, NIV)

Here, Jesus is giving a lesson to his disciples. The truth of the matter is, you are blessed for all the suffering that you go through in this life as long as you have Jesus as your savior. You are building your reward for your life. God promises your assurance that you are his, and he will protect you through all obstacles in your life.

My sheep listen to my voice; I know them, and they follow me. I give them eternal life, and they shall never perish; no one will snatch them out of my hand. My Father, who has given them to me, is greater than all; no one can snatch them out of my Father's hand. I and the Father are one. (John 10:27–30, NIV)

No matter what, you have been saved and are Jesus's sheep. No one can lead you astray if you stay with your Savior. Whenever you feel like you're away from God, always take a look back at your life. Don't ever be afraid to go back to the basics and always ask yourself the following:

- Am I reading the Bible daily?
- Am I praying?
- Am I asking for forgiveness?
- What am I doing with what God has given me?
- Am I helping others?
- Am I feeding my own selfish needs or the needs of God?

What, then, shall we say in response to these things? If God is for us, who can be against us? He who did not spare his own Son, but gave him up for us all—how will he not also, along with him, graciously give us all things? Who will bring any charge against those whom God has chosen? It is God who justifies. Who then is the one who condemns? No one. Christ Jesus who died—more than that, who was raised to life—is at the right hand of God and is also interceding for us. Who shall separate us from the love of Christ? Shall trouble or hardship or persecution or famine or nakedness or danger or sword?

As it is written:

"For your sake we face death all day long; we are considered as sheep to be slaughtered."

No, in all these things we are more than conquerors through him who loved us. For I am convinced that neither death nor life, neither angels nor demons, neither the present nor the future, nor any powers, neither height nor depth, nor anything else in all creation, will be able to separate us from the love of God that is in Christ Jesus our Lord. (Romans 8:31–39, NIV)

How powerful is the above verse. Your faith in Jesus is more than the anxieties of the world. Nothing can separate you from your Savior. Do not let fear control your destiny. Fear is the lack of love and trust in Jesus Christ, and that's it. Here are some things you should never fear because the world says to. The reason is this, God's promise says not to:

- Death
- Life
- Angels
- Demons
- Past
- Bills
- Family

IMMANUEL

- Present
- Future
- Any power
- Anything in all creation

> There is no fear in love. But perfect love drives out fear, because fear has to do with punishment. The one who fears is not made perfect in love. (1 John 4:18, NIV)

> Praise be to the God and Father of our Lord Jesus Christ! In his great mercy he has given us new birth into a living hope through the resurrection of Jesus Christ from the dead, and into an inheritance that can never perish, spoil or fade. This inheritance is kept in heaven for you, who through faith are shielded by God's power until the coming of the salvation that is ready to be revealed in the last time. In all this you greatly rejoice, though now for a little while you may have had to suffer grief in all kinds of trials. These have come so that the proven genuineness of your faith—of greater worth than gold, which perishes even though refined by fire—may result in praise, glory and honor when Jesus Christ is revealed. Though you have not seen him, you love him; and even though you do not see him now, you believe in him and are filled with an inexpressible and glorious joy, for you are receiving the end result of your faith, the salvation of your souls. (1 Peter 1:3–9, NIV)

God's promise is so profound that we couldn't even fathom the reason.

1. Are you suffering?
2. Do you not understand why things are the way they are?
3. Are you unhappy with your life?
4. Do you feel that the world is against you?

If you have answered yes to any of these questions, then you are not alone. You are one of God's chosen to inherit the kingdom of God. Welcome to God's army.

> The people who walked in darkness have seen a great light. They lived in the land of shadows, but now light is shining on them. You have given them great joy, Lord; you have made them happy. They rejoice in what you have done, as people rejoice when they harvest grain or when they divide captured wealth. For you have broken the yoke that burdened them and the rod that beat their shoulders. You have defeated the nation that oppressed and exploited your people. (Isaiah 9:2–4, NIV)

If you are always planning evil, you will earn a reputation as a troublemaker. Any scheme a fool thinks up is sinful. People hate a person who has nothing but scorn for others. (Proverbs 24: 10)

LEAP Challenge 23

Today you will not live in fear for God's promise to us. Go out and enjoy the day, and share the Word of God with others. Give them the same gift that was offered to you. It doesn't matter if it is to one person or to a hundred people; the goal is to go and share this precious gift. Make a list at the bottom of this paper of all the people you have shared God's Word with.

L.E.A.P. Insight

> A wise old owl sat on an oak; the more he saw the less he spoke; the less he spoke the more he heard; why can't we be like that wise old bird.
>
> —Unknown Author

Mind

1 Thessalonians Chapter 2

1. T or F _____ Paul and other followers had previously suffered and been treated outrageously in Philippi, but with the help of our God we dared to tell you his gospel in the face of strong opposition. (2)

> Once when we were going to the place of prayer, we were met by a female slave who had a spirit by which she predicted the future. She earned a great deal of money for her owners by fortune–telling. She followed Paul and the rest of us, shouting, "These men are servants of the Most High God, who are telling you the way to be saved." She kept this up for many days. Finally Paul became so annoyed that he turned around and said to the spirit, "In the name of Jesus Christ I command you to come out of her!" At that moment the spirit left her. When her owners realized that their hope of making money was gone, they seized Paul and Silas and dragged them into the marketplace to face the authorities. They brought them before the magistrates and said, "These men are Jews, and are throwing our city into an uproar by advocating customs unlawful for us Romans to accept or practice." The crowd joined in the attack against Paul and Silas, and the magistrates ordered them to be stripped and beaten with rods. After they had been severely flogged, they were thrown into prison, and the jailer was commanded to guard them carefully. When he received these orders, he put them in the inner cell and fastened their feet in the stocks. (Acts 16:19–24)

2. For you,_____, became imitators of God's churches in Judea, which are in Christ Jesus: You suf-

fered from your own people the same things those churches suffered from the Jews. (14)

> But other Jews were jealous; so they rounded up some bad characters from the marketplace, formed a mob and started a riot in the city. They rushed to Jason's house in search of Paul and Silas in order to bring them out to the crowd. (Acts 17:5)

3. Who killed the Lord Jesus and the prophets and also drove us out? Who displeased God and are hostile to everyone in their effort to keep us from speaking to the Gentiles so that they may be saved?

> After many days had gone by, there was a conspiracy among the Jews to kill him, but Saul learned of their plan. Day and night they kept close watch on the city gates in order to kill him. (Acts 9:23–24)

Mind Meditation Checklist

25 Minutes

> I am with you and will watch over you wherever you go, and I will bring you back to this land. I will not leave you until I have done what I have promised you. (Genesis 28:15, NIV)

- Find a quiet, comfortable place. Sit in a chair or on the floor with your head, neck, and back straight, but not stiff.
- Put aside all thoughts of the past and the future, and stay in the present. Focus on the verse above.

IMMANUEL

- Become aware of your breathing. With every breath you take allow, your body to be filled with the Holy Spirit.
- Scan your body, starting with your feet, and work your way up, always ending with your head.
- Focus on the sensation of air moving in and out of your body as you breathe. Release all your sin as you exhale, and invite all of God's Spirit as you inhale.
- Pay attention to the way each breath changes and is different.
- Watch every thought of sin, worry, fear, anxiety, or hate come into your mind, and release it with every exhale.
- When any thoughts come up in your mind, don't ignore or suppress them but simply observe them, remaining calm and collected, giving them all to the Lord.
- If you find yourself getting carried away in your thoughts, just focus back on Jesus and simply return to your breathing, inhaling the Holy Spirit with every breath.
- Remember, do not be hard on yourself when you lose focus. You are just beginning a pure form of godly meditation.
- Now as the time comes to a close, sit for a minute or two, becoming aware of where you are, and get up gradually.

L.E.A.P. 27

Body

L.E.A.P 27 Daily Workout Log

Date (Day/Month/Year): _____

Start Time: _____

End Time: _____

Scale Weight:	
Body Fat %:	
Fitness Goal:	Strength/Muscle Building/Fat Loss/Endurance/Other:

Body Parts Trained (Circle all that apply):

Whole Body | Chest | Back | Shoulders | Legs | Calves | Biceps | Triceps | Abs | Other: _____

CARDIO/AEROBIC/CONDITIONING EXERCISE

EXERCISE	TIME	DISTANCE/INTENSITY

WEIGHT, STRENGTH & RESISTANCE TRAINING

EXERCISE	WEIGHT	SETS	REPS	REST	NOTES

DIET & NUTRITION

MEAL	FOODS EATEN	APPROXIMATE CALORIES
BREAKFAST:		
LUNCH:		
DINNER:		

SELF EVALUATION

OVERALL WORKOUT RATING (1-10)		IMPROVEMENT NOTES:	

Day 24

FOLLOW BY EXAMPLE

Daily Verse

Follow my example, as I follow the example of Christ. (1 Corinthians 11:1, NIV)

Therefore if you have any encouragement from being united with Christ, if any comfort from his love, if any common sharing in the Spirit, if any tenderness and compassion, then make my joy complete by being like-minded, having the same love, being one in spirit and of one mind. Do nothing out of selfish ambition or vain conceit. Rather, in humility value others above yourselves, not looking to your own interests but each of you to the interests of the others. In your relationships with one another, have the same mindset as Christ Jesus:

Who, being in very nature God, did not consider equality with God something to be used to his own advantage; rather, he made himself nothing by taking the very nature of a servant, being made in human likeness. And being found in appearance as a man, he humbled himself by becoming obedient to death—even death on a cross! Therefore God exalted him to the highest place and gave

IMMANUEL

him the name that is above every name, that at the name of Jesus every knee should bow, in heaven and on earth and under the earth, and every tongue acknowledge that Jesus Christ is Lord, to the glory of God the Father.

Do Everything Without Grumbling

Therefore, my dear friends, as you have always obeyed—not only in my presence, but now much more in my absence—continue to work out your salvation with fear and trembling, for it is God who works in you to will and to act in order to fulfill his good purpose. Do everything without grumbling or arguing, so that you may become blameless and pure, "children of God without fault in a warped and crooked generation." Then you will shine among them like stars in the sky as you hold firmly to the word of life. And then I will be able to boast on the day of Christ that I did not run or labor in vain. But even if I am being poured out like a drink offering on the sacrifice and service coming from your faith, I am glad and rejoice with all of you. So you too should be glad and rejoice with me. (Philippians 2:1–18, NIV)

Leading by example is the best way to show the world that you are a different person through Jesus. This is not a "Do what I say" life but a "Do what I do" life. When you put the whole program together, you will officially *love* everyone because Jesus loves you; *enjoy* every moment 'cause time will pass; *accept* any situation 'cause no matter what, something is going to happen, and you can't control it; and *praise* God and give peace all by your own personal actions. It is time for you to live the walk and not just boast about it.

It was just before the Passover Festival. Jesus knew that the hour had come for him to leave this world and go to the Father. Having loved his own who were in the world, he loved them to the end. The evening meal was in progress, and the devil had already prompted Judas, the son of Simon Iscariot, to betray Jesus. Jesus knew that the Father had put all things under his power, and that he had come from God and was returning to God; so he got up from the meal, took off his outer clothing, and wrapped a towel around his waist. After that, he poured water into a basin and began to wash his disciples' feet, drying them with the towel that was wrapped around him. He came to Simon Peter, who said to him, "Lord, are you going to wash my feet?" Jesus replied, "You do not realize now what I am doing, but later you will understand." "No," said Peter, "you shall never wash my feet." Jesus answered, "Unless I wash you, you have no part with me." "Then, Lord," Simon Peter replied, "not just my feet but my hands and my head as well!" Jesus answered, "Those who have had a bath need only to wash their feet; their whole body is clean. And you are clean, though not every one of you." For he knew who was going to betray him, and that was why he said not everyone was clean. When he had finished washing their feet, he put on his clothes and returned to his place. "Do you understand what I have done for you?" he asked them. "You call me 'Teacher' and 'Lord,' and rightly so, for that is what I am. Now that I, your Lord and Teacher, have washed your feet, you also should wash one another's feet. I have set you an example that you should do as I have done for you. Very truly I tell you, no servant is greater than his master, nor is a messenger greater than the one who sent him. Now that you know these things, you will be blessed if you do them. (John 13:1–17, NIV)

Jesus is the Son of God, and yet he washed his disciples' feet. Why would he do such a thing? His reasoning was to lead by example. He could have told them to go and do it for others, but

IMMANUEL

he showed them that no matter who you are, you must always lead others by example. Imagine the impact you would make in the world if your actions surpassed your own words.

You live in a world where technology surpasses humanity. Humanity was always created way before technology. It is time to exceed in your true nature and overcome soulless devices. It all starts with you, and it will end with you.

If you are weak in a crisis, you are weak indeed. (Proverbs 24:11–12)

LEAP Challenge 24

Today, go out and be that example that Jesus set for you. Do not use your words to express to others your glory; better yet, use your actions to show them the way toward the truth.

"It's time to stop talking about being for Jesus, and learn to just be like Jesus in your actions."

L.E.A.P Insight

Jesus said, "Forgive one another." Isn't it funny how we add to God's word? Now we added "forget." The main focus is man's word, not God's word. We've all been asked, "How do you know if you have truly forgiven a person"; and the response time and time again is "By forgetting all their harm they committed to me." The truest form of forgiving in its purity is the love and actions you show to the people who have sinned against you.

For what is easier, to say your sins be forgiven; or to say arise and walk? But that you may know that the Son of man has power on earth to forgive sins, then said to the sick, Arise take your bed and go to your house (Matthew 9: 5–6, NIV).

Anyone can say, "I will forgive and forget," but can you "forgive and be the physical miracle in your enemies eyes."

| 270 |

Mind

1 Thessalonians 3

1. Who did Paul send to strengthen and help the church in Thessalonica? (1–3) _____

   Those who escorted Paul brought him to Athens and then left with instructions for Silas and Timothy to join him as soon as possible. (Acts 17:15)

2. But Timothy has just now come to us from you and has brought good news about your _____ and _____. (6)

Mind Meditation Checklist

25 Minutes

   I also saw under the sun this example of wisdom that greatly impressed me: There was once a small city with only a few people in it. And a powerful king came against it, surrounded it and built huge siege works against it. Now there lived in that city a man poor but wise, and he saved the city by his wisdom. (Ecclesiastes 9:13–15, NIV)

- Find a quiet, comfortable place. Sit in a chair or on the floor with your head, neck, and back straight, but not stiff.
- Put aside all thoughts of the past and the future, and stay in the present. Focus on the verse above.
- Become aware of your breathing. With every breath you take, allow your body to be filled with the Holy Spirit.
- Scan your body, starting with your feet, and work your way up, always ending with your head.

IMMANUEL

- Focus on the sensation of air moving in and out of your body as you breathe. Release all your sin as you exhale, and invite all of God's Spirit as you inhale.
- Pay attention to the way each breath changes and is different.
- Watch every thought of sin, worry, fear, anxiety, or hate come into your mind, and release it with every exhale.
- When any thoughts come up in your mind, don't ignore or suppress them but simply observe them, remaining calm and collected, giving them all to the Lord.
- If you find yourself getting carried away in your thoughts, just focus back on Jesus and simply return to your breathing, inhaling the Holy Spirit with every breath.
- Remember, do not be hard on yourself when you lose focus. You are just beginning a pure form of godly meditation.
- Now as the time comes to a close, sit for a minute or two, becoming aware of where you are, and get up gradually.

L.E.A.P. 27

Body

L.E.A.P 27 Daily Workout Log

Date (Day/Month/Year): _____

Start Time: _____

End Time: _____

Scale Weight:	
Body Fat %:	
Fitness Goal:	Strength/Muscle Building/Fat Loss/Endurance/Other:

Body Parts Trained (Circle all that apply):

Whole Body | Chest | Back | Shoulders | Legs | Calves | Biceps | Triceps | Abs | Other: _____

CARDIO/AEROBIC/CONDITIONING EXERCISE

EXERCISE	TIME	DISTANCE/INTENSITY

WEIGHT, STRENGTH & RESISTANCE TRAINING

EXERCISE	WEIGHT	SETS	REPS	REST	NOTES

DIET & NUTRITION

MEAL	FOODS EATEN	APPROXIMATE CALORIES
BREAKFAST:		
LUNCH:		
DINNER:		

SELF EVALUATION

OVERALL WORKOUT RATING (1-10)		IMPROVEMENT NOTES:	

Day 25

PETER AND YOU

Daily Verse

> The third time he said to him, "Simon son of John, do you love me?" Peter was hurt because Jesus asked him the third time, "Do you love me?" He said, "Lord, you know all things; you know that I love you." Jesus said, "Feed my sheep. (John 21:17, NIV)

What is the difference between Peter, one of Jesus's disciples, and you? Peter was the most famous of the disciples. But he was famous not because he was the smartest or because he never did anything wrong; he was famous because he had the most faith! How did Peter get such great faith? By trying to live by the words of Jesus, but it was not easy. Sometimes Peter succeeded, and sometimes he failed in his walk, but each success, and especially each failure, strengthened his faith.

In Luke 5:4, Jesus told Peter, "Put out your nets for a catch." Peter answered, "Master, we've worked all night and haven't caught anything. But because you say so, I will let down the nets."

When they had done so, they caught such a large number of fish that their nets began to break. When Peter saw this, he fell at Jesus's knees and said, "Go away from me, Lord; I am a

| 275 |

IMMANUEL

sinful man!" But Jesus said to him, "Don't be afraid; from now on you will be a fisher of men." So they left everything and followed Jesus. Here is a success of Peter. Peter believed in Jesus and obeyed his commands, and Jesus showed him a miracle.

You

You are no different. How many times has Jesus asked you to do something and it sounded so absurd that you didn't listen? Just imagine if you did.

Peter

In another story in Matthew 14:25, the disciples were in a boat at night in a storm. Jesus went out to them, walking on the water. When the disciples saw Jesus, Peter said, "Lord, order me to come to you on the water." Jesus said, "Come." So Peter started to walk on the water. But when he saw the wind, he became afraid, and in the midst of sinking, he cried out, "Lord, save me!" Immediately Jesus caught him and helped him into the boat. Then he asked Peter, "Why did you doubt?" Peter was successful when he started walking on the water, but he lost his faith, and his success turned into a failure.

You

Have you ever had such a success in something that even when things are going right, you don't know why they are? Then you sabotage yourself to sink back down to where you feel comfortable. You have the ability to overcome any success in your life with Jesus in your life. Even when you sink, if you just call on the Lord, he will reach out his hand and pull you to safety. When you put your trust in Jesus, he will have you walk on water, and if your faith falters, he will reach for you. All you have to do is call out for him.

Peter

In another story, in Matthew 16:13, Jesus asked his disciples, "Who do people say I am?" Peter answered, "You are the Christ, the Son of the living God." Jesus said, "Blessed are you, Peter for this was not revealed to you by man, but by my Father in heaven. And I tell you that on the rock of your faith in Me, I will build my church." Peter succeeded yet again. He accurately identified Jesus as the Son of God.

You

You have already established that Jesus is the Son of God. Welcome to your ultimate success in your life.

Peter

In another story, in Luke 22:31, Jesus said to Peter, "Satan will put you to the test, but I have prayed that when you have turned back to Me again, you will strengthen your brethren." Peter said, "Lord, I am ready to go with you to prison and even to death." Jesus said, "I tell you, Peter, the cock will not crow this day, until you deny that you know me three times."

In Matthew 26: 69, it says that later that night, Peter entered the courtyard, and a servant said, "You were with Jesus." But Peter denied it before them all. Then he went out to the gateway, where another girl saw him and said, "This fellow was with Jesus." He denied it again, this time with an oath: "I don't know this man!" A while later, other people said, "Surely you are one of them, for your accent gives you away." Then he denied it with curses and swore, "I don't know this man!" Immediately a rooster crowed, and Peter remembered what Jesus said about the rooster, and he went outside and wept bitterly.

Why did Peter fail? Peter was a natural leader who had faith in his own strength. But the church of Jesus could be built not on the strength of Peter but on total faith in Jesus. Only when Peter failed 100 percent and lost all faith in himself could he put all of his faith in Jesus. Jesus can build a church on anyone of us who has 100 percent of our faith in Jesus.

In Mark 16:1, on the third day after Jesus's death, the women went to the tomb. But the body of Jesus was gone, and an angel was there, who said, "Jesus has risen! Go tell his disciples and Peter." The angel purposely mentioned Peter. Jesus was reaching out to Peter in Peter's failure. These words assure us that our failures need never be the end of a relationship with our Savior.

Judas also failed Jesus that night, and he ended his life. Peter was ashamed of his behavior, but he hung in there through the pain. Although he had abandoned Jesus, a part of Peter knew that Jesus wouldn't abandon him.

You

How many times have you failed Jesus? Can you count the ways on your hands? Probably not, but that is the greatest thing about Jesus. He will never abandon you even if you turned your back on him.

Peter

In Acts 3:1, after Jesus had ascended into heaven, Peter and John entered the temple. A man crippled from birth asked them for money. Peter said, "Silver or gold I do not have, but what I have I give you. In the name of Jesus Christ, get up and walk." Then Peter pulled him up, and instantly, the man's feet and ankles became strong, and he began to walk. The man went with them into the temple courts, walking and jumping and praising God. Peter's faith in Jesus brought him a success (Acts 4:5). But the next day, Peter and John were brought before the authorities. They asked Peter by what power he healed the paralytic. Peter, filled with the Holy Spirit, said to them, "The man was healed by the power of Jesus Christ, whom you crucified but whom God raised from the dead."

When the leaders saw the courage of Peter, they were astonished, but they commanded him not to teach in the name of Jesus. But Peter replied, "Judge for yourselves whether it is right in God's sight to obey you rather than God. For we cannot help speaking about what we have seen and heard." But after further threats, the authorities let Peter and John go.

You

You can have the faith of Peter through your failures. It takes all your failures in life to create 100 percent faith in God. Your faith is with Jesus, and he has sent you his Holy Spirit to guide you on your path.

Peter and You

Peter and you had many successes and failures in life. But Peter did not allow his failures to determine an ending relationship with Jesus. And it can be the same with you. You will fall down from time to time. But when you do, Jesus asks you to get back up, brush yourself off, and continue forward. He encourages you to keep your faith and continue living the kingdom lifestyle.

Don't hesitate to rescue someone who is about to be executed unjustly. You may say that it is none of your business, but God knows and judges your motives. He keeps watch on you; he knows. And he will reward you according to what you do. (Proverbs 24: 13–14)

LEAP Challenge 25

Today you have learned that you are no different from Peter. You will succeed and fail, but it is your actions that you take when you do fail. When you live the kingdom of heaven lifestyle today, challenge yourself to keep your faith in Jesus. And if you fail today, just pick yourself up and build your faith upon the failures of your life.

Turn all your failures into a life of success in Jesus's name.

L.E.A.P. Insight

The Son will turn CONVICTIONS to be His Fathers GRACE.
The Son will turn FAILURES to be His Fathers SUCCESSES.
The Son will turn DEFEAT to be His Fathers VICTORY.
The Son will turn HISTORY to be His Fathers LEGACY.

The Son will turn DESTINY to be His Fathers MEMORY.
In Return
The Father will turn DEATH to be His Son's RESURRECTION.

"All things have been committed to me by my Father. No one knows who the Son is except the Father, and no one knows who the Father is except the Son and those to whom the Son chooses to reveal him." Luke 10:22 NIV

Mind

Thessalonians Chapter 4

1. T or F _____ It is God's will that you should be sanctified: that you should never avoid sexual immorality; that each of you should learn not learn to control your own body in a way that is holy and honorable. (3–4)

   > But as for the Gentiles who have become believers, we have sent them a letter telling them we decided that they must not eat any food that has been offered to idols, or any blood, or any animal that has been strangled, and that they must keep themselves from sexual immorality. (Acts 21:25)

2. For we believe that Jesus _____ and _____ again, and so we believe that God will bring with Jesus those who have fallen asleep in him. (15)

   > Listen to this secret truth: we shall not all die, but when the last trumpet sounds, we shall all be changed in an instant, as quickly as the blinking of an eye. For when the trumpet sounds, the dead will be raised, never to die again, and we shall all be changed. (1 Corinthians 15:51–52)

Mind Meditation Checklist

25 Minutes

> But Jesus immediately said to them: "Take courage! It is
> I. Don't be afraid." "Lord, if it's you," Peter replied, "tell
> me to come to you on the water." "Come," he said. Then
> Peter got down out of the boat, walked on the water and
> came toward Jesus.30 But when he saw the wind, he
> was afraid and, beginning to sink, cried out, "Lord, save
> me!" Immediately Jesus reached out his hand and caught
> him. "You of little faith," he said, "why did you doubt?"
> (Matthew 14:27–31, NIV)

- Find a quiet, comfortable place. Sit on a chair or on the floor with your head, neck, and back straight, but not stiff.
- Put aside all thoughts of the past and the future, and stay in the present. Focus on the verse above.
- Become aware of your breathing. With every breath you take, allow your body to be filled with the Holy Spirit.
- Scan your body, starting with your feet, and work your way up, always ending with your head.
- Focus on the sensation of air moving in and out of your body as you breathe. Release all your sin as you exhale, and invite all of God's Spirit as you inhale.
- Pay attention to the way each breath changes and is different.
- Watch every thought of sin, worry, fear, anxiety, or hate come into your mind, and release it with every exhale.
- When any thoughts come up in your mind, don't ignore or suppress them but simply observe them, remaining calm and collected, giving them all to the Lord.
- If you find yourself getting carried away in your thoughts, just focus back on Jesus and simply return to your breathing, inhaling the Holy Spirit with every breath.

IMMANUEL

- Remember, do not be hard on yourself when you lose focus. You are just beginning a pure form of godly meditation.
- Now as the time comes to a close, sit for a minute or two, becoming aware of where you are, and get up gradually.

Body

<u>L.E.A.P 27 Daily Workout Log</u>

Date (Day/Month/Year): _____

Start Time: _____

End Time: _____

Scale Weight:	
Body Fat %:	
Fitness Goal:	Strength/Muscle Building/Fat Loss/Endurance/Other:

Body Parts Trained (Circle all that apply):

Whole Body | Chest | Back | Shoulders | Legs | Calves | Biceps | Triceps | Abs | Other: _____

CARDIO/AEROBIC/CONDITIONING EXERCISE

EXERCISE	TIME	DISTANCE/INTENSITY

WEIGHT, STRENGTH & RESISTANCE TRAINING

EXERCISE	WEIGHT	SETS	REPS	REST	NOTES

DIET & NUTRITION

MEAL	FOODS EATEN	APPROXIMATE CALORIES
BREAKFAST:		
LUNCH:		
DINNER:		

SELF EVALUATION

OVERALL WORKOUT RATING (1-10)		IMPROVEMENT NOTES:	

Day 26

TIME FOR EVERYTHING

Daily Verse

When evening comes, you say, "It will be fair weather, for the sky is red," and in the morning, "Today it will be stormy, for the sky is red and overcast." You know how to interpret the appearance of the sky, but you cannot interpret the signs of the times. (Matthew 16:2–3, NIV)

There is a time for everything, and a season for every activity under the heavens:

a time to be born and a time to die,
a time to plant and a time to uproot,
a time to kill and a time to heal,
a time to tear down and a time to build,
a time to weep and a time to laugh,
a time to mourn and a time to dance,
a time to scatter stones and a time to gather them,
a time to embrace and a time to refrain from embracing,
a time to search and a time to give up,
a time to keep and a time to throw away,

IMMANUEL

a time to tear and a time to mend,
a time to be silent and a time to speak,
a time to love and a time to hate,
a time for war and a time for peace.

What do workers gain from their toil? I have seen the burden God has laid on the human race. He has made everything beautiful in its time. He has also set eternity in the human heart; yet no one can fathom what God has done from beginning to end. I know that there is nothing better for people than to be happy and to do good while they live. That each of them may eat and drink, and find satisfaction in all their toil—this is the gift of God. I know that everything God does will endure forever; nothing can be added to it and nothing taken from it. God does it so that people will fear him. (Ecclesiastes 3:1–14, NIV)

In this day and age, there is a time for everything. No matter what you do from this moment till one hour from now, there is something that is going to happen. You cannot control the time. All you can do is just accept it. This is your time to show the world how unique and special you are. Always remember, God has his own special time for everything. You just have to enjoy and accept the time given to you. Take advantage of the time that was given to you, and share the joy and happiness with others.

It is time for you to act, Lord; your law is being broken. (Psalm 119:126, NIV)

When times are good, be happy; but when times are bad, consider this: God has made the one as well as the other. Therefore, no one can discover anything about their future. (Ecclesiastes 7:14, NIV)

For there is a proper time and procedure for every matter, though a person may be weighed down by misery. (Ecclesiastes 8:6, NIV)

You see, at just the right time, when we were still powerless, Christ died for the ungodly. (Romans 5:6, NIV)

The eyes of all look to you, and you give them their food at the proper time. (Psalm 145:15, NIV)

My child, eat honey; it is good. And just as honey from the comb is sweet on your tongue, you may be sure that wisdom is good for the soul. Get wisdom and you have a bright future. (Proverbs 24:15–16)

L.E.A.P. Challenge

Today, you are going to experience all that time has to offer you. Embrace each moment today and let nothing pass you by. Hold on to every event that happens to you today and write it in your journal so you can realize how amazing God's time is.

L.E.A.P. Insight

What's so funny is the excuse that we all love: "There is just never enough time in the day" to do anything. We all tend to use that excuse almost every day until God made a bold statement: "My Son had the same twenty-four hour day that you have, and He changed the world." Now what is your excuse?
Mind

Hebrews Chapter 1

1. You are my_____; today I have become your _____.
   (5)

| 285 |

I will be his father, and he will be my son. When he does wrong, I will punish him with a rod wielded by men, with floggings inflicted by human hands. (2 Samuel 7:14)

2. T or F_____ Gods firstborn he will say "Let all God's angels worship him." (6)

Rejoice, you nations, with his people, for he will avenge the blood of his servants; he will take vengeance on his enemies and make atonement for his land and people. (Deuteronomy 32:43, NIV)

3. He makes his_____ spirits, and his _____ flames of fire. (7)

He makes winds his messengers, flames of fire his servants. (Psalm 104:4)

4. T or F _____ God you have hated the righteousness and loved the wickedness. (9)

You love righteousness and hate wickedness; therefore God, your God, has set you above your companions by anointing you with the oil of joy. (Psalm 45:7)

5. Who laid the foundations of the earth? (10–12)

_____

In the beginning you laid the foundations of the earth, and the heavens are the work of your hands. They will perish, but you remain; they will all wear out like a garment. Like clothing you will change them and they will be discarded. But you remain the same, and your years will never end. (Psalm 102:25–27)

6. What side did God tell his son Jesus to sit on? (13)

The Lord says to my lord: "Sit at my right hand until I make your enemies a footstool for your feet." (Psalm 110:1)

Mind Meditation Checklist

25 Minutes

But I trust in you, Lord; I say, "You are my God." My times are in your hands; deliver me from the hands of my enemies, from those who pursue me. Let your face shine on your servant; save me in your unfailing love. (Psalm 31:14–16, NIV)

- Find a quiet, comfortable place. Sit in a chair or on the floor with your head, neck, and back straight, but not stiff.
- Put aside all thoughts of the past and the future, and stay in the present. Focus on the verse above.
- Become aware of your breathing. With every breath you take, allow your body to be filled with the Holy Spirit.
- Scan your body, starting with your feet, and work your way up, always ending with your head.
- Focus on the sensation of air moving in and out of your body as you breathe. Release all your sin as you exhale, and invite all of God's Spirit as you inhale.
- Pay attention to the way each breath changes and is different.
- Watch every thought of sin, worry, fear, anxiety, or hate come into your mind, and release it with every exhale.
- When any thoughts come up in your mind, don't ignore or suppress them but simply observe them, remaining calm and collected, giving them all to the Lord.

IMMANUEL

- If you find yourself getting carried away in your thoughts, just focus back on Jesus and simply return to your breathing, inhaling the Holy Spirit with every breath.
- Remember, do not be hard on yourself when you lose focus. You are just beginning a pure form of godly meditation.
- Now as the time comes to a close, sit for a minute or two, becoming aware of where you are, and get up gradually.

L.E.A.P. 27

Body

L.E.A.P 27 Daily Workout Log

Date (Day/Month/Year): _____

Start Time: _____

End Time: _____

Scale Weight:	
Body Fat %:	
Fitness Goal:	Strength/Muscle Building/Fat Loss/Endurance/Other:

Body Parts Trained (Circle all that apply):

Whole Body | Chest | Back | Shoulders | Legs | Calves | Biceps | Triceps | Abs | Other: _____

CARDIO/AEROBIC/CONDITIONING EXERCISE

EXERCISE	*TIME*	DISTANCE/INTENSITY

WEIGHT, STRENGTH & RESISTANCE TRAINING

EXERCISE	*WEIGHT*	*SETS*	*REPS*	*REST*	*NOTES*

DIET & NUTRITION

MEAL	*FOODS EATEN*	*APPROXIMATE CALORIES*
BREAKFAST:		
LUNCH:		
DINNER:		

SELF EVALUATION

OVERALL WORKOUT RATING (1-10)		IMPROVEMENT NOTES:	

Day 27

WATCHMEN (TESTIFY, IT'S YOUR TURN NOW)

Daily Verse

Religion that God our Father accepts as pure and faultless is this: to look after orphans and widows in their distress and to keep oneself from being polluted by the world. (James 1:27, NIV)

At the end of seven days the word of the Lord came to me: "Son of man, I have made you a watchman for the people of Israel; so hear the word I speak and give them warning from me. When I say to a wicked person, 'You will surely die,' and you do not warn them or speak out to dissuade them from their evil ways in order to save their life, that wicked person will die for their sin, and I will hold you accountable for their blood. But if you do warn the wicked person and they do not turn from their wickedness or from their evil ways, they will die for their sin; but you will have saved yourself. "Again, when a righteous person turns from their righteousness and does evil, and I put a stumbling block before them, they will die. Since

IMMANUEL

you did not warn them, they will die for their sin. The righteous things that person did will not be remembered, and I will hold you accountable for their blood. But if you do warn the righteous person not to sin and they do not sin, they will surely live because they took warning, and you will have saved yourself." The hand of the Lord was on me there, and he said to me, "Get up and go out to the plain, and there I will speak to you." So I got up and went out to the plain. And the glory of the Lord was standing there, like the glory I had seen by the Kebar River, and I fell facedown. Then the Spirit came into me and raised me to my feet. He spoke to me and said: "Go, shut yourself inside your house. And you, son of man, they will tie with ropes; you will be bound so that you cannot go out among the people. I will make your tongue stick to the roof of your mouth so that you will be silent and unable to rebuke them, for they are a rebellious people. But when I speak to you, I will open your mouth and you shall say to them, 'This is what the Sovereign Lord says.' Whoever will listen let them listen, and whoever will refuse let them refuse; for they are a rebellious people. (Ezekiel 3:16–27, NIV)

It is your turn to be a watchman for Christ. The Lord Almighty is coming, and he is waiting for you to announce it. It is time to prepare his people and wait for his coming. From this day forth, you must do two major parts in your new walk. The first you must ask yourself is what the first thing Jesus Christ ever said was.

And He said to them, "Why did you seek Me? Did you not know that I must be about My Father's business?" (Luke 2:49, NKJV)

Finally, ask yourself what was the last thing that Jesus Christ says in the Bible.

L.E.A.P. 27

So when Jesus had received the sour wine, He said, "It is finished!" And bowing His head, He gave up His spirit. (John 19:30, NKJV)

Notice the two most important words that Jesus had left for you to guide your walk in him. Every morning when you arise you must be doing God's business and right before you go to bed you need to ask yourself, is it truly finished. Will you be ready to do Gods work?

A prophecy against Dumah: Someone calls to me from Seir, "Watchman, what is left of the night? Watchman, what is left of the night?" The watchman replies, "Morning is coming, but also the night. If you would ask, then ask; and come back yet again." (Isaiah 21:11–12, NIV)

Listen! Your watchmen lift up their voices; together they shout for joy. When the Lord returns to Zion, they will see it with their own eyes. Burst into songs of joy together, you ruins of Jerusalem, for the Lord has comforted his people, he has redeemed Jerusalem. The Lord will lay bare his holy arm in the sight of all the nations, and all the ends of the earth will see the salvation of our God. (Isaiah 52:8–10, NIV)

Stand at the crossroads and look; ask for the ancient paths, ask where the good way is, and walk in it, and you will find rest for your souls. But you said, "We will not walk in it." I appointed watchmen over you and said, "Listen to the sound of the trumpet!" But you said, "We will not listen." Therefore hear, you nations; you who are witnesses, observe what will happen to them. Hear, you earth: I am bringing disaster on this people, the fruit of their schemes, because they have not listened to my words and have rejected my law. (Jeremiah 6:16–19, NIV)

IMMANUEL

The best of them is like a brier, the most upright worse than a thorn hedge. The day God visits you has come, the day your watchmen sound the alarm. Now is the time of your confusion. Do not trust a neighbor; put no confidence in a friend. Even with the woman who lies in your embrace guard the words of your lips. For a son dishonors his father, a daughter rises up against her mother, a daughter-in-law against her mother-in-law—a man's enemies are the members of his own household. But as for me, I watch in hope for the Lord, I wait for God my Savior; my God will hear me. (Micah 7:4–7, NIV)

Don't be glad when your enemies meet disaster, and don't rejoice when they stumble. The Lord will know if you are gloating, and he will not like it; and then maybe he won't punish them. (Proverbs 24:17–18)

LEAP Challenge 27

Today is the day that you will put together all that you have learned over the next 27 days. Today you will live like a rooster. I know what you're thinking: "What does that mean?" Well, actually, take a look at a rooster's demeanor. They hold their head up high and walk with grace and pride. Yet when they get their daily bread, they bow down humbly to eat. Now you know the true meaning of being a rooster.

L.E.A.P. Insight

Don't worry about how sharing God's Word will make you look. It is unimportant what the "world" thinks of you. If you are obedient to the promptings of the Holy Spirit when He is giving you the desire to share God's Word, then go for it.

The apostle Paul said: "For I am not ashamed of the Gospel of Christ, for it is the power of God unto salvation, to everyone who believes."

He who wins souls is wise!

So, let me encourage you—go for it and take a stand! If you don't believe in anything, you will truly fall for everything.

Mind Meditation Checklist

30 Minutes

> Therefore, since we are surrounded by such a great cloud of witnesses, let us throw off everything that hinders and the sin that so easily entangles. And let us run with perseverance the race marked out for us, fixing our eyes on Jesus, the pioneer and perfecter of faith. For the joy set before him he endured the cross, scorning its shame, and sat down at the right hand of the throne of God. Consider him who endured such opposition from sinners, so that you will not grow weary and lose heart. (Hebrews 12:1–3, NIV)

- Find a quiet, comfortable place. Sit in a chair or on the floor with your head, neck, and back straight, but not stiff.
- Put aside all thoughts of the past and the future, and stay in the present. Focus on the verse above.
- Become aware of your breathing. With every breath you take, allow your body to be filled with the Holy Spirit.
- Scan your body, starting with your feet, and work your way up, always ending with your head.
- Focus on the sensation of air moving in and out of your body as you breathe. Release all your sin as you exhale, and invite all of God's Spirit as you inhale.
- Pay attention to the way each breath changes and is different.
- Watch every thought of sin, worry, fear, anxiety, or hate come into your mind, and release it with every exhale.

IMMANUEL

- When any thoughts come up in your mind, don't ignore or suppress them but simply observe them, remaining calm and collected, giving them all to the Lord.
- If you find yourself getting carried away in your thoughts, just focus back on Jesus and simply return to your breathing, inhaling the Holy Spirit with every breath.
- Remember, do not be hard on yourself when you lose focus. You are just beginning a pure form of godly meditation.
- Now as the time comes to a close, sit for a minute or two, becoming aware of where you are, and get up gradually.

L.E.A.P. 27

Body

L.E.A.P 27 Daily Workout Log

Date (Day/Month/Year): _____

Start Time: _____

End Time: _____

Scale Weight:	
Body Fat %:	
Fitness Goal:	Strength/Muscle Building/Fat Loss/Endurance/Other:

Body Parts Trained (Circle all that apply):

Whole Body | Chest | Back | Shoulders | Legs | Calves | Biceps | Triceps | Abs | Other: _____

CARDIO/AEROBIC/CONDITIONING EXERCISE

EXERCISE	TIME	DISTANCE/INTENSITY

WEIGHT, STRENGTH & RESISTANCE TRAINING

EXERCISE	WEIGHT	SETS	REPS	REST	NOTES

DIET & NUTRITION

MEAL	FOODS EATEN	APPROXIMATE CALORIES
BREAKFAST:		
LUNCH:		
DINNER:		

SELF EVALUATION

OVERALL WORKOUT RATING (1-10)		IMPROVEMENT NOTES:	

About the Author

> If the world hates you, just remember that it has hated me first. (John 15:18, NIV)

> "Is not my word like fire," declares the Lord, "and like a hammer that breaks a rock in pieces?" (Jeremiah 23:29, NIV)

Well, where to begin? This book is a complete memoir of my life transformation when I was in jail for back-to-back DUIs and an aggravated assault charge. This book started as just a simple journal for me to get by one day at a time and look at the positive insight on why I was there. I didn't belong there, or did I? In this part of the book, I will show you that God is merciful and loving. You will know my deepest secrets that are an important part of how God made this all possible.

My Revelation

It took a lot for me to understand that God created me, not my parents. I was a part of a greater plan than just my birth.

> I am the Lord who created you; from the time you were born, I have helped you. Do not be afraid; you are my servant, my chosen people whom I love. (Isaiah 44:2, NIV)

IMMANUEL

I always seemed to struggle with all aspects of my life. It all started with my personality. I wasn't raised on how to love one another; I just had to know. We never said it in the household, and it was hard to grasp the concept of telling my own father, mother, and brother that I love them. Due to not knowing how to love, I lost so much in my life. I pushed away anyone who ever cared about me, including my ex and my son. I turned something that was supposed to be special and loving into repressed anger and hate, which led to a very long road of depression. I can honestly say I had been depressed for quite a long time. At least over ten years of my life. I never had a purpose in life and had no self-confidence. The only real trait that I ever portrayed in my life was I was proficient in lying. I was able to manipulate any situation in my favor. I had many different personalities in my life that I had to create in order to please everyone whom I was around with. I never knew who I truly was. Who was Manuel Gonzalez?

I suffered from an addictive nature. Binge drinking was all I knew. Drinking in moderation was not in my vocabulary. Drugs also played a role in my life. Even though I got into so much trouble, I would still pound alcohol until I blacked out, not knowing if I would wake up the next morning. Who knows, maybe in reality I was committing slow and painful suicide on myself.

My background wasn't any better. From when I was a child till ninth grade, I have no recollection of what happened in my life. I just have slight pictures in my head, almost like a slide show of still pictures. None of them make any sense, but who knows? I've always masked and lied about everything that I created a world that my imagination developed to escape certain parts of my life. Only God truly knows.

As for my appearance, I have always been self-conscious of my appearance. I used to weigh over 240 pounds and felt uneasy about it. Even when I lost all the weight and was 165 pounds, I still saw that troubled heavyset man staring back at me. There were times I couldn't even look at my own eyes in the mirror. I never was sure what I was disappointed in more: the way I looked or the way I felt about the way I looked. Talk about a double-edged sword in my life. Notice the quote below. It describes my nature. In my eyes, it is insanity in a nutshell.

> Part of every misery is, so to speak, the misery's shadow or reflection: the fact that you don't merely suffer but that you have to keep on thinking about the fact that you suffer. I not only live each endless day in grief, but I live each day thinking about living each day in grief. (C. S. Lewis)

My faults were these: I always wanted someone's approval, and I love to drink alcohol. The only time I ever felt good was when I was told "Wow, you're a marine" or "You are in good shape, you look good," and even "I'm proud of you." These are the earthly things I was looking for in my life.

My drinking was the major focal point of my depression. I knew I needed to stop, but the temptation was so great. The answer was so simple: just stop drinking. That is what my loved ones would always say. It's so simple, right? Wrong. This part of my life is the destruction part. From tearing up previous relationships, to hurting my progress in the military, to hurting my family and—the worst thing I could have ever faced in my life—to losing my own sons' respect for me as a father and knowing they are terrified of me. I had three Public Intoxications, three Driving While Intoxicated, and an Aggravated Assault—all pending. Yes, that is how much alcohol destroyed my life, but why?

I could always remember what my sons' mother would tell me: "You are cheating on me with your mistress." And only in time could I tell that she was so right. Alcohol was my mortal enemy and would be my demise if I continued. There was never an explanation for why I did what I did. I fell into the simple worldly excuses in life: maybe it's hereditary, it's a disease, or— my favorite excuse of all time—"I was never taught how to drink responsibly." It never mattered what excuse I used. The bottom line was, alcohol was the master of my life and I was its servant. It had total control of my life, and if I didn't change soon, it would control the outcome of my death. Ten years of my life had come and, in a blink of an eye, gone away. "What did I accomplish during this time?" All I do know are the bad decisions I had made during my drinking.

Now it was time to come to the acceptance part of my life. I only had two choices, and no more.

1. Blame everyone but myself on why I was sitting in a jail cell.

For the first choice, I came to recognize that kind of thinking led me to anger and animosity toward the people I loved.

2. Face the complete conviction head on and accept my mistakes.

At this instant, I knew this was the answer to my problem, but how do I change what I've been doing for over a decade?

It took me thirty-three years, a lot of trials and tribulations, heartaches, and pain to others that I loved to finally understand my purpose in this life. God has always wanted me to walk in his grace, but I was too blinded by my own desires. As a parent who disciplines their children, God had to discipline me. He didn't do it out of anger but out of compassion because he knew he could use me for a greater good.

> Have you forgotten the encouraging words which God speaks to you as his sons?
>
> "My son, pay attention when the Lord corrects you, and do not be discouraged when he rebukes you. Because the Lord corrects everyone he loves, and punishes everyone he accepts as a son."
>
> Endure what you suffer as being a father's punishment; your suffering shows that God is treating you as his sons. Was there ever a son who was not punished by his father? (Hebrews 12:5–7, NIV)

The truth was always slapping me in the face, yet I was blinded by the lies of the flesh and bone. I always felt the presence of God all around me, but I just never comprehended the unconditional love he had for me. The craziest part of this journey was that I was so scared to pick up the Bible and read it. I was even terrified to pray. Not because I was afraid there was no God or that he wouldn't answer my prayers. That wasn't it at all. As a matter of fact, it was the opposite. I was scared that he would answer my prayers, and the trials and tribulations that follow, I would not be strong enough to overcome them. It took just one verse to change my way of thinking.

> This is all that I have learned: God made us plain and simple, but we have made ourselves very complicated. (Ecclesiastes 7:29, NIV)

What a shock to find out that I was conflicted not because of God but because I had complicated my life to the fullest, and that was the truth. That verse to me was a wake-up call for my mission to have God make my life uncomplicated. Live for God; it's that plain and simple.

The Change

Imprisonment changed my life. I was given the opportunity to read the entire New Testament and the start of the Old Testament. I am a living, breathing example that the Bible and the experiences I had to go through to understand that God's Word is truly the alive. While I was sitting in my cell, God touched my heart and soul and opened my eyes to a new approach to witnessing God's love. While I was in jail, I took the opportunity to witness to other prisoners about what I was trying to do with this journal I had. At the time, that was all it was, just a simple journal that God touched and spoke through, and turned into this terrific 27-day God-based transformation.

IMMANUEL

When I was in there, I really wasn't sure whether or not God had touched their lives through me. The one thing I was sure of was that I planted a seed into their hearts and let God do the rest. The truth of the matter was I was happy to spread this joy in my life with others and couldn't wait to see them prosper in a new light.

Now don't get me wrong. I have had my own personal struggles. I was never perfect in my life, but that is the most amazing testimony that I could give about my Savior, Jesus Christ. He truly knows that I was never perfect. He never asked me to be perfect, but I felt obligated to try to be. I failed every time and put myself in a depression. I couldn't see the big picture in my life that God was trying to show me. The answer was so simple: Jesus died on the cross for my sins. Why couldn't I just accept this wonderful gift of salvation?

Another startling discovery is the statements that our Savior made in Matthew, Mark, Luke, and John. These changed my life forever. It was like the words came alive and spoke to me off the page. Take a look at the bottom passages, and let me explain myself.

> At noon the whole country was covered with darkness, which lasted for three hours. At about three o'clock Jesus cried out with a loud shout, "Eli, Eli, lema sabachthani?" which means,
>
> "My God, My God, why did you abandon me?" (Matthew 27:45–46, NIV)

> At noon the whole country was covered with darkness, which lasted for three hours. At three o' clock Jesus cried out with a loud shout, "Eloi, Eloi, lema sabachthani?" which means,
>
> "My God, My God, why did you abandon me?" (Mark 15:33–34, NIV)

Jesus knew that by now everything had been completed; and in order to make the scripture come true, he said, "I am thirsty." A bowl was there, full of cheap wine; so a sponge was soaked in the wine, put on a stalk of hyssop, and lifted up to his lips. Jesus drank the wine and said, "It is finished!" then he bowed his head and gave up his spirit. (John 19:28–30, NIV)

These three passages are what opened my eyes to God's purpose for my life. First, in Matthew, Mark, and Luke, it states three times how darkness covered the country. This is the way I felt in my own personal life. Darkness was covering my world, and I didn't know how to get out. I came to realize that even darkness tries to cover the light.

When doubts filled my mind, your comfort gave me renewed hope and cheer. (Psalm 94:19, NIV)

Second, it says Jesus cried out, "My God, My God, why did you abandon me?" Jesus Christ was as human as you and me in an emotional state. I felt the same feelings and emotions that Jesus did. In my time of gloom, I cried out with all my heart. Why was I abandoned in my darkest time? Why was I in jail when I don't deserve to be here? Was this a punishment? Could you imagine how many times Paul asked this same question when he was locked away in jail?

My God, my God, why have you abandoned me? I have cried desperately for help, but still it does not come. (Psalm 22:1, NIV)

Third, notice how Jesus knew that the prophecy, even though He felt abandoned, was almost whole, and in order to complete God's Word, he said, "I am thirsty." Then they sponged cheap

IMMANUEL

wine and gave it to him. This is interesting to me. Christ said, "I am thirsty," and the first reaction as a man was to offer a drink. But was Jesus thirsty for a worldly item, or was he calling out to the Father that his spirit was thirsty? Think about it. In my life, I was tired of living in the darkness and asking God why. That was all I did. "Why this?" or "Why that?" was always coming from my mouth. Instead of asking the Father to fill my spirit, I was asking God why and then seeking answers from others. I chose worldly answers and not the answers of God. Then I realized that Jesus, even though he felt alone and the darkness covered over him, had a purpose to fulfill God's promise. He never lost sight of that. Jail made me realize that I had lost sight of God's purpose in my life and I needed to be in that place of darkness, not as punishment but as an awakening. Even though I was in a dark place, my purpose was very clear and was brought into the light: to write this book and to share the love and peace that God has instilled in my own personal life through the dark moments.

> When I was hungry, they gave me poison; when I was thirsty, they offered me vinegar. (Psalm 69:21, NIV)

> My throat is as dry as dust, and my tongue sticks to the roof of my mouth. You have left me for dead in the dust. (Psalm 22:15, NIV)

> It was about twelve o' clock when the sun stopped shining and darkness covered the whole country until three o' clock; and the curtain hanging in the Temple was torn in two. Jesus cried out in a loud voice, "Father! In your hands I place my spirit!" He said this and died. (Luke 23:44–46, NIV)

The final piece of this remarkable revelation was the completion of God's plan. Notice how there are two important parts in this passage.

L.E.A.P. 27

1. The curtain hanging in the Temple was torn in two.

In Exodus, it shows what the curtain represents.

> Make a curtain of fine linen woven with blue, purple and red wool. Embroider it with figures of winged creatures. Hang it on four posts of acacia wood covered with gold, fitted with hooks, and set in four silver bases. Place the curtain under the row of hooks in the roof of the tent, and put the Covenant Box containing the two stone tablets behind the curtain. The curtain will separate the Holy Place from the Most Holy Place. (Exodus 26:31–33, NIV)

This curtain was used to separate the place of worship from the law. When Jesus died for our sins, he gave us a way out from the law of God. God's law was made to describe and hold me accountable for my sins. And God's love was given to me when Christ died and overcame the law. I could never understand that if you live by the law, you die by the law. But the compassion of God gave me a way out from the law. His name is Jesus Christ.

2. In the above passage, Jesus cries out, "Father! In your hands I place my spirit!" and when he said this, he gave his spirit to the Father.

When I read this second part, I realized that I had to do the same. I had to place my spirit in his hands. As Christ died on the cross and his spirit ascended into heaven, my sins died on that same cross and my spirit rose to heaven. I was redeemed by God's grace, and his Son took my place on that cross. I gained so much knowledge and wrote this book, and have been given a second chance at life to share God's love and compassion.

Jesus has always been the teacher, but I was never the student. Jesus has always led by example, and it was time for me to follow in his footsteps. In John 13:1–20, notice how our Savior washes

| 307 |

IMMANUEL

his disciples' feet. He showed that even though he is the Son of God, there needs to be humility and he is to lead by example.

> I, your Lord and Teacher, have just washed your feet. You, then, should wash one another's feet. I have set the example for you, so that you will do just what I have done for you. I am telling you the truth: no slave is greater than his master, and no messenger is greater than the one who sent him. Now that you know this truth, how happy you will be if you put it into practice. (John 13:14–17, NIV)

Jesus didn't just tell his disciples do what he says. He told them to do what he does. During these revelations, I was taught and was willing to share my gift through this book. This was my process that I had to follow to get close to God.

- Humble myself. Understand that I am not greater than Jesus and I needed him in my life no matter what.
- Ask for forgiveness. I needed my soul cleansed and needed Jesus in my heart.
- Jesus sends me his Holy Spirit. My old spirit was renewed with the Holy Spirit. That is why this book is possible.

This was when I realized I can walk with Christ and truly search for my purpose in this world. I realized I was just a simple piece to a marvelous puzzle called life. Just like any puzzle, if one piece is lost, the whole puzzle can't ever be complete. I didn't want to be that lost piece but instead wanted to be a small piece of God's great masterpiece.

In closing, I just have to say that I have stared at my past long enough that my future started to pass me by. Only then was when I sat down and wondered where Manuel Gonzalez has been all these years. It is time to live for today because yesterday has already passed and tomorrow is not here yet, but today, I will live for the glory of God in Jesus Christ's name.

L.E.A.P. 27

And always remember, Christians never meet for the last time!

> There will be the shout of command, the archangel's voice, the sound of God's trumpet, and the Lord himself will come down from heaven. Those who have died believing in Christ will rise to life first; then we who are living at that time will be gathered up along with them in the clouds to meet the Lord in the air. And so we will always be with the Lord. (1 Thessalonians 4:16–17, NIV)

> Listen to this secret truth: we shall not all die, but when the last trumpet sounds, we shall all be changed in an instant, as quickly as the blinking of an eye. For when the trumpet sounds, the dead will be raised, never to die again, and we shall all be changed. (1 Corinthians 15:51–52, NIV)